T0196486

BREATHE ONLY LOVE

A PATH TO GOD'S PRESENCE

JOHN M. COLES

WESTBOW
PRESS®
A DIVISION OF THOMAS NELSON
& ZONDERVAN

Scripture quotations taken from the New American Standard Bible® (NASB),
Copyright © 1960, 1962, 1963, 1968, 1971, 1972, 1973, 1975, 1977, 1995 by
The Lockman Foundation Used by permission. www.Lockman.org

WestBow Press books may be ordered through booksellers or by contacting:

WestBow Press
A Division of Thomas Nelson & Zondervan
1663 Liberty Drive
Bloomington, IN 47403
www.westbowpress.com
1 (866) 928-1240

ISBN: 978-1-5127-6635-6 (sc)
ISBN: 978-1-5127-6636-3 (hc)
ISBN: 978-1-5127-6634-9 (e)

Library of Congress Control Number: 2016919620

Print information available on the last page.

WestBow Press rev. date: 11/23/2016

DEDICATION

This book is dedicated to my four children: Anjeanette Coles Damon, Barbara Coles Zinda, Kevin Coles, and Karen Coles Rosvall. To know how great your contributions of love to our communities are is truly one of the greatest accomplishments a parent could ask for. As is the case, I have been a different father to each of you, due to the changes occurring as time passes and other factors. Hopefully this book communicates to you the power of God's love in our lives as a family and the part of your father that you all have in common.

CONTENTS

ACKNOWLEDGMENTS

First and foremost, there is one person who has empowered this book to come about. This is my wife, who is my life's love. She has remained married to me for over four decades and through raising four children. She has more than validated my theory that love is a choice, granted to us by God, and sustained by His Son. In addition to her love, she has transcribed this entire book from tapes I've lectured into. She then proofread the book over five times—I've lost count. As a more indirect contribution from her, she raised a child who proofread the book and identified an essential missing ingredient. Barbara told me to include my life experiences with my theories. Thank you, Kathleen Coles and Barbara Zinda.

Next are the countless students of mine over the last thirty-five years who have asked me, "When are you going to write a book? You should!" Okay, I finally believed you guys! My place of employment, Truckee Meadows Community College, provided me with the means to teach about love from the psychological angle. Along with them are others who both proofread and critiqued my work. Dick Williams ironed out most of my grammatical errors. Ron Bell, a playwright and counselor, identified my inconsistencies in speaking to my readers. Nadine Phinney compiled my bibliography, which was no small task.

A very special acknowledgment goes to Virginia Castleman, a highly successful author and college adjunct professor of English.

She has guided me through the ins and outs of using metaphors, using proper grammar, and negotiating who to select for a self-publisher. In addition, I thank her for providing a second sense of urgency for "getting this message out there."

The first to be acknowledged for lighting the fire under me to get this done are people in Catholic/Christian ministry. Francisca Gonzalez, Outreach Coordinator for Christ the King Retreat Center, paved the way for my first Heart of the Christian retreat in Citrus Heights, California. She gave me the opportunity to test my theories of developing a deeper spirituality in the faithful. Thanks to Auguste Lemaire, who attended my first talk and retreat. Deacon Augie has supported me and encouraged me from the beginning. Finally, I give strong acknowledgment to Fr. David Geib of the St. Benedict Retreat and Conference Center in Mckenzie River, Oregon. He has provided Kathleen and me with a steady spiritual influence since our college days. His review of this work pointed out the importance of not putting my ideas forth as *the path* to God, but as one of many paths. This distinction is not only intuitively and theologically correct, but supported by the brain research that he motivated me to discover.

Thank you all, and thank you to all the others who I don't have the space to thank.

AUTHOR'S NOTE

I once went up to my minister after his sermon and said, "Do you know that you mentioned the heart in each of your last three sermons to us?" He indicated that he wasn't aware of that. I then asked him, "Were you referring to our actual, physiological hearts, or were you referring to our hearts metaphorically?" He responded that it was metaphorical, of course. Whereupon, I suggested that Christianity could well be served by looking at the biblical references on the heart as physiological. He then pulled out his concordance and was astonished to see how many references to the heart were found in the Bible. He thumbed through page after page of biblical references in the concordance.

I was already writing this book to explore the physiological aspects of the heart in the Bible when I approached my minister with this idea. I've always been a person who was trained in logic but who preferred the minutiae of everyday living. I was taught in childhood how to prove the existence of God through the use of logic. But I always believed that the proof was just experiencing God—like experiencing people in general. My hope with this book is to lead you through the obscurities of everyday Christian living toward a simpler existence of inviting God into your experience of life.

Those obscurities that I referred to are simply the life experiences that are causing so many of us to be stressed. Having been a stress management expert for over three decades, I am fully aware of how stress interferes with thinking, with health, and with spiritual living. I've also been vividly aware of how stress appears to be winning the battle over relaxation in our society. What I didn't know was that relaxation is not the best goal for stress management. There are many people with aroused nervous systems who are both spiritual and not ruining their health. I hope to show you that the secret to stress management is a loving heart. By "loving heart," I mean a physiological heart of love.

As a college professor, I've often heard my students suggest that I write a book. My response has usually been that I'd write a book as soon as I could speak to something original. Certainly, if this topic is found in the Old Testament of the Bible, it is not original. And the Bible tells us not to be stressed. What I'm also hoping to convey with this book is how psychology and the Bible each have something to offer to the other. Recently, psychology has been discovering the role of breathing and heart rate changes in stress management. When I first began teaching how to actually practice this approach for stress management, I noticed that it also appeared to be triggering some people's spiritual lives. Reading scripture gave me the insight of how the Bible validated this recent neurological research. One of the answers to neutralizing the non-Christian forces in our lives appears to be the amazingly simple skill of breathing only love.

PART 1

Defining the Challenge

CHAPTER 1

To Love or Not to Love

In many ways, lives enter, exit, and reenter the light. I know that my life has been that way. I remember my childhood as dark, with rare moments of seeing things more in line with the way they really were. To an outside observer of my life, I had everything. But inside of me was psychological pain, sorrow, and fear. I hungered for those moments when the shadows would fade and joy and security would enter my life. Those moments would come when very special people would relate to me. These people had twinkles in their eyes and appeared to me to be enlightened. My forty-plus years of being a therapist have taught me that I was far from alone in my fear, even though I felt that way.

Perhaps the gradual exposure to enlightened people in my life was meant to result in a lifelong pursuit of understanding those twinkles in their eyes. As my awareness of those relationships grew over the years, I learned that what I saw is called *love*. And just as darkness attempts to overrule light, some who use the word *love* merely use it to do anything but love their fellow men and women. To see the true brilliance of love, we need to face the darkness head-on and make some hard choices. Let's explore that darkness first and then the flickering light of choices. Finally, we can then view the brilliance of love in all its simplicity!

To begin, as most views of love do, I'll ask questions. For

1

instance, you might ask, "Does a person even want to consider a life of loving?" I think that questions like "why love?" and "what will someone get out of it, if someone does love?" are key questions for all of us if we are to come out of the shadows of aloneness and unawareness. The desire to benefit from love seems contrary to love. The main question is a lot deeper than just "why love?" By this I mean, how do you or I even define love? Does *love* in your mind mean the same that it means in mine? There are so many things that are done in the name of love that love itself becomes incomprehensible amid the many uses of the term.

Leo Buscaglia (1972) once said that love is one of those words that is so big that it can't be defined. He said that the only word that he can find that's even close to love is *life*. So now the question might become, is life love? What will a person get out of it if he or she does love? There are a lot of people who think that love is just a bunch of mushy words for poets and songwriters, that there's very little to it that's objective, and that it's like a mirage that fades away. A person pursues the image of the mirage, enveloped by yearning, longing, lusting, and desiring. And while pursued, it's just fine. Euphoric, even. Then, just as mysteriously as it came, it disappears, leaving that person feeling lost, lonely, cheated, and confused.

Love can be hard. Love is often painful. When you look at the pain and the heartache that come from choosing to love, then the question "why love?" has a whole lot deeper connotation to it.

What makes entering into a life of love worth the pain it involves? What makes love worth enduring the uncertainty of even understanding it accurately at all? Why would somebody pursue this shiny illusion of light, especially if someone showed him or her the pain, uncertainty, and even heartache? Part of the mystery is that even those who do enter into the brightness of love often seem to get blinded by it anyway. So again. Why love?

And why do so many—who don't want that heartbreak—make those same mistakes over and over and over again? Why do so many stay in relationships that are dark, harmful, and destructive when they are in pursuit of a love that can't really be objectively defined or verified? That's a very hard question for me to answer. I think that the answer is more than just a paragraph or the first chapter of a book. "Life" questions usually are. We'll need a little help.

Poets write about fantastic feelings that come with love. Indeed, when I was studying for my counseling psychology degree, there was a poster in the Counselor Education Department that said, "Feelings are like a faucet: both the hot water and the cold water come out of the same spigot." The meaning of the metaphor becomes instantly clear: if we turn off the painful, destructive feelings, we also turn off the fulfilling, wonderful, beautiful, warm feelings that we could have had. Unfortunately, we live in a world that taxes love so strongly that we get hurt very deeply. With some people, the invitation to love causes an automatic, knee-jerk reaction to just shut down and go numb when the opportunity to love arises. This is really unfortunate, because that faucet closes to the wonders of love as well. And the result is that we become numb, blind, and dead inside. The extent of this dynamic is vast.

I'll share how I see what this internal pain is doing to modern culture. I don't speak of culture here in the sense of really fantastic, wonderful works of art and of fantastic expressions in music or theater that are coming forth. I mean the culture found in the everyday lives of citizens in this world.

If we were to ask people in our culture to generally describe what they are feeling, I suspect they are going to say that they are *frustrated*. That word seems to describe the cultural psyche that is so predominant in this twenty-first century, and it interrupts the potential to live a life of love. Statistics show that road rage has emerged at a level much higher than it has before (Sharkin 2004). Although statistics show a decline in college student suicides (Sharkin 2004), statistics do show that violent crime is prevalent, with 95 percent of high schools across the country having at least one violent crime (Gregory, et al. 2010). Frustration is behind a lot of these statistics. Frustration can be hurtful. If I need something and the media electronically dangles it in front of me on a regular basis as a kind of fantasy, I feel the frustration. I feel the frustration because the "carrot" is realistically unavailable. It's like a mirage that surprises me by vanishing.

Like me, people are led to believe that the fantasy is obtainable just by watching television or listening to another form of media. If I need love, and every time that I get close to loving, a stoplight turns red and stops me from bathing in the sunlight of love, that frustration of returning to that hurt time and time again becomes huge in proportion. I think that we can apply this frustration to all of the human needs here. It could be hunger for food. It could be the need to be on time. Frustration takes every opportunity to foil our plans. It is also one of the major kinds of stress.

According to the study of stress management, when an individual is hit by one great big stressor, the human body is designed to deal with it. The history of humanity has given biology a built-in reaction to crisis, known as the fight-or-flight response. The crises that our species experienced in the past required an increased use of muscles and other physiological processes in order to stay and fight a threat or to flee the threat. Today, we need a psychological defense in our everyday lives, yet we're still restricted to this fight-or-flight response.

Although these big stressors certainly occur today, what's really causing tension and frustration in modern culture is a series of tiny interruptions in whatever people are intending. You may intend to get just a half hour more sleep, for example. You may not know that, because you're asleep. Yet, you *need* one more half hour of sleep. Then—*blast*—some fast-talking radio announcer is telling you about war across the seas. Or—*boom*—your first experience on morning radio is some mass death from a catastrophe. Or—heaven forbid—it's a story about a psychotic murderer who succeeded in some atrocity. By inviting the interruption, you and I start our days right off with frustration instead of loving feelings.

So you stumble out of bed, and you get into the shower to just vegetate in that moment of bliss pouring upon you. Then, another family member turns on his or her shower of intended blissful vegetation. Your water goes from just the right temperature to either too freezing or too hot. And—*boom*—you have that same reaction in the body that was designed for a life-threatening situation. Now you've had two stressful experiences—and a half hour hasn't even gone by.

Year after year, each individual adds just a little bit more exhaustion to his or her life. So he or she gets to the point where maybe caffeine or nicotine is added for energy. In a lot of cases, some engage in drug abuse in order to bring them up past that level of exhaustion—where they can face the demands destined to hit them on any given day.

If you look at a newspaper, what do you read? "Fantastic act of love just occurred yesterday"? No, you don't read that. You read about the latest violence. First, the radio may be getting to you. Now the printed word is confronting you as well.

You climb into your car, pull out of your driveway, and proceed to a street where traffic is buzzing by you. Where you used to have, maybe, fifty feet to pull in front of a car, now you've got fifteen feet at best—and you better step on it quickly, or else you'll be just sitting there. The people in the cars behind you may be getting frustrated and upset at you. Some will even sound the horn. You get on the freeway, and *bam*. There's the road rage and a new sense of injustice when somebody cuts you off on the freeway! Fess up. Do you talk—maybe even yell—from inside your car at a guy in the car in front of you who frankly couldn't care less, and can't hear you anyway? I do! I just have to express something, even if no one is listening, to help relieve some of the frustration.

And then you get to work.

The workplace is often depicted as impersonal and as rabidly in the pursuit of profit for somebody else. This contributes to the breaking down of relationships and family. I often spend so much of my energy focused on the workplace. Many modern workers are even finding love relationships in the workplace (Sills 2007). And nowadays, if they're not finding love in the workplace, they jump online. Maybe you are someone who looks for love through a machine that asks questions. If so, you'd need to rely on a computer program to screen out the people for you to consider for loving. If you aren't pursuing love through this approach, odds are that you know someone who is. Don't get me wrong—a lot of good can come from an effective machine working in harmony with true values. The point is that you and I probably have so many demands being placed upon us in our fast-paced, demand-for-convenience lives that even our love is being pressured for mechanization.

As with any symptomatic situation, causes and effects occur.

What has happened to modern societies, where there aren't enough healthy interactions between people so that love grows naturally out of face-to-face reactions? Is love to become electronic? Something mechanical? Perhaps even battery operated? Have societies started down that path? How convenient, how efficient, and how devoid of feeling is this? Is this the price paid to feel safe with feelings? I believe that love in the world has entered a twilight, a half-love of dark aloneness and of light of another person relating through our computer screens.

If so, how safe are feelings?

I don't think most people feel safe today. I think the average person is safer than is realized, but due to these stressors coming at them, and due to a deficit of love, people may be feeling more threatened psychologically than they care to admit. Does this apply to you?

Look at this rapid, insane living for profit that we have. We have how many televisions in our houses? How many computers? How many cars? Has love transferred to objects? How many times have you heard others say things like, "I love that outfit," or "I love this game."

Today, I hear the words, "human resources," a lot. The words are often used with "natural resources" or "material resources"— like all people should be lumped together with objects. Don't we need to be doing just the opposite of treating people like things? Doesn't the will to be loving require us to not treat one another as means to an end? All that time spent "loving" by acquiring!

How many hours per week have you spent to get a second television? How afraid are you to turn to the person with whom you partnered and build something together in face-to-face interaction? Even if you decide to connect, look at how much time you'd have to spend to sustain the creativity necessary for your decision. It requires depth of being. I believe that it requires a daily spontaneity to recreate yourself as a gift to your partner. One of the deepest fears is the fear of looking inside and seeing nothing but a deep, dark abyss, a void of anything to offer another.

I feel amazed at how much people run from that fear of what they're going to find inside. Think for a moment. How many feelings of pain have been shut off, not experienced, and therefore, not finished? These shut-off feelings still reside in the neuron pathways of nervous systems of bodies and brains. These shut-off feelings seem to be still waiting for similar situations to come up. These new situations may cause most feelings to shut off as well, and thus one does not have to look inside and face the darkness.

This fear of looking inside brings to mind the idea that humanity may come to an end without giving it a fight—a sort of apathetic and meaningless giving up. Can someone, as a person, shrivel to the point where he doesn't even exist anymore? Would someone even want to? Some, who call themselves visionaries, look down this rather dark road and view this as the very definition of tomorrow's humanity.

Indeed, there are currently people in various fields arguing that humanity needs to leave the biological sphere (Cohen 2013) by pulling out of the body and adding any number of replacements, including fake skin, fake muscle, prosthetic hands, arms, legs, feet, noses, pancreases—the list goes on. Some believe that they would be making the body more efficient. And from there, all of the violence, war, killing, pain, and hurt that is inflicted upon humanity will cease, because feelings will be eliminated, including feelings that feed war.

Perhaps that's your future as a member of the human race. Do you want that? I don't. Discussion is already taking place to have a link between the human brain and a computer in order to augment the human brain (Cohen 2013). What if you could download everything from your brain into a computer? They're talking about a future with nanotechnology, as well: injecting tiny, atom-sized machines into bodies to perform functions. Doctors could use nano-machines to go to the part of the brain causing depression and zap it, so that the depression wouldn't be there anymore. Does this sound inviting? I view these ideas as attempts to mechanize love itself.

Is it possible that the future will have a point where people will not be able to distinguish between where biology stops and machine inventions begin? Well, this is scary. A lot of times, after the progress becomes part of our daily lives, we're not scared anymore. Sometime, that's better; sometimes not. As an example, fear is needed when danger is real and imminent.

So, another question arises: Will people head toward dying—biological nonexistence—without a fight in a quagmire of self-inflicted apathy? Or will people live, fighting for who they are by thrusting a stake into the ground and saying to the world, "This is who I am?" "Take me for who I am." "Enhance who I am." First, there is a choice to be a person of identity. Then, that person may choose to love or not to love. It very well could be that as a race, the pain of looking inside at the hurts of yearning for love is the first step on a path to our future existence!

What is the status of the average person today? Is it one of frustration, of one irritant right after another? It's not as bleak as that. You still have wonderful movies. You still have wonderful novels. Art is still a tremendous industry in this country. You still have many people who see the light of love on the freeway that are not cutting off each other. In so many ways, the people around us are a compilation of confusing opposites, like we're watching both a sunset and a sunrise at the same time.

One of the earliest psychologists, Carl Jung, said that individuation—which was his word for a personality becoming fully blossomed into its best potential—involves integrating opposites (Jung 1962). This integration of our opposites is kind of like that water spigot I saw in my doctoral department office. You and I are tender, and you and I are violent. There are so many opposites to who we are.

CHAPTER 2

OPPOSITE ANGELS

When I was a young child wrestling with whether I was really "a bad boy" or not, I went to my mother and asked her if I was bad. Her response was that I had two angels assigned by God to me that were on my shoulders. One of those angels was very, very bad. She said that he whispered in my ear to always do bad things, like teasing my sister. If I listened to him and followed his suggestions, I would wind up cranky, mad, guilty, and full of the sin of pride. If I followed this angel, I'd also wind up not getting to go to heaven. I told my mother that this was scary, and she said that yes it was, but that I also had another angel.

When I asked about the other angel, she said that it would also be on my other shoulder whispering into my ear. This good angel would always tell me to do good things, like helping my sister when she needed it. If I listened to him and followed his suggestions, I would wind up happy, calm, and innocent and be a humble little boy. If I followed this angel, I'd go to heaven.

She could see how very puzzled I must have looked, so she asked me what was wrong. My answer was that I was afraid of not going to heaven to be with God. She indicated that it was up to me to choose which angel to listen to and that God gave that power of choosing to me. Which one would I choose? It was up to me.

Once you see the glimmer of the sunrises of love in your life, you have a choice to make of whether to listen to and follow that love or not. These opposites inside of you, and inside me as a curious little boy, appear in all cultures. In the Chinese philosophy of Tai Chi the yin and the yang represent the balance between the dark and the bright. Dualities abound in the pioneering work of Carl Jung, who said that we have within us, both introversion and extroversion. There are so many different kinds of dualities and opposites (Jung 1962).

Jung (1962) says that, to develop fully as a human being, I need to kiss the snake. In other words, I need to look at both the positive and the negative sides of myself. I need to look at both my positive and my negative feelings. Why love, if I must kiss this snake, kiss what my mother called the devil inside me? I don't like snakes, and I don't like this negative side of me. Maybe I can go halfway but not as far as embracing or kissing this side of me. Wouldn't this be going over to the dark side of not loving at all?

Are you afraid that you're going to look inside yourself and see a black, unending abyss? Are you a black hole of nothingness? Isn't it ironic that it's through that abyss and that it's by kissing that snake that you can find the good that is in you, the love? You could find peace, joy, and love. You could choose which angel inside of you to listen to, if you only knew these two sides better.

If most of what you call evil within comes from the hurt you bestow on others and receive from others, then psychology needs to look at that hurt. Psychology needs to deal with it in a kind, gentle, and loving manner, so that the highest side of human nature can shine forth. Psychology needs to nurture more people like Einstein, Gandhi, and Robert Kennedy on this planet.

You have this ability, this sunlight, within you now. You can choose to enhance it and brighten it and shine it on your freeways and on your workplace. It's such a hard question to look at. The question was, "Why love?" There are so many answers to this question—so many directions it could take us. And we need to find and own our own reasons for living a life of love.

So, why love? Perhaps it's because thousands of years ago somebody loved. Love wouldn't even exist if someone hadn't loved before. Why love? Perhaps it's because your grandma loved you. How many grandmas love or don't love somebody? There are many reasons why we can love.

Approaching love rationally by asking "why" is one path. I prefer a path of asking, "How?" "*How* do we love?" is a better question for what I choose to teach here. How do we love on our freeways? How do we love in the workplace? How do we go through that abyss, kiss the snake, and love ourselves? Not "Why?" The question for my style of loving becomes, "How?"

"How?"

This was the question when I worked with a woman who had failed in mathematics six times, all forms of mathematics, such as math in business, and taking courses in math itself. Every time she was presented with a math problem in a classroom situation, she would just freak out. Everything inside of her was frustrated, angry, hurt. How could she love herself while presented with a math problem?

Every time math reared its ugly head into her life, she would go into that response, and she would shut down. Her brain would cease to think clearly. Now, there's a reason for "why love?" right there. Do you want the clear-thinking part of your brain to shut down when you need it? Because if you shut out self-love, that's what's going to happen. In the course of working on it, she hit on a memory that later she realized was the source of why she avoided math so much.

In third grade, she was belittled by a teacher. She missed several days of classes. When she returned, she was told to go to the board and do a math problem, when she had no clue how to do the math problem. The teacher started belittling her in front of the whole class, making the class laugh, forcing her to stand at the blackboard through all the breaks. She even had to stand there during the lunch break. She wasn't allowed to go to the bathroom.

An hour after class her mother found her still standing there. Her mother came for her because she hadn't walked home after class. She then had to face the embarrassment of being exposed for her "stupidity"—ignorance called stupidity—in front of her mother. *Decades* went by before she could do math again. What was she to do?

She needed to look inside, and instead of running away from that frustration, instead of running away from that pain and hurt, she needed to look at it straight in the eye. She lived in a world where there were very few avenues where you can go kiss the snake. It's a skill, kissing a snake. And I guess that's one of the first things I want to spotlight about love, in terms of trying to define the undefinable: love is also a skill.

Love is referred to as both a feeling that I have inside and as a behavior I implement. So when I say, "I love you," I'm saying that there's a feeling inside of me called love that I'm sending forth to you. But love is also a skill. If I say, "I love you," with a shouting and angry tone of voice, then I may have the feeling of love inside of me, but I'm not employing a skill of loving you. Feeling and skill are two different things. Perhaps that's why so many people fall in and out of love so often. The feelings come, and the skills to love have never been bred into a habit of behavior that is available for implementation. Then people perpetually wonder why they always hurt the ones they love. If the skills for loving were there, then the choice would be there.

And so, if we're now a populace struggling to find these skills for love, how can we begin to even love ourselves? How can we kiss a snake that is representing fear, frustration, and anger? These are the kinds of emotions depicted in the Bible as evil. Why would we look and embrace something that's evil? The answer is that it depends on whether we choose to love or not to love. But we need to acknowledge both forces inside us in order to choose which one to act with.

I don't believe that the majority of today's citizenry is

consciously choosing to feed anger and frustration. While some are, I think they're more entrapped by it. I think it has taken many of them over—this culture of anger and frustration. They do not have the skills to love themselves in an angry, frustrating situation. They don't have the skills to develop that depth of personality to bring forth a new and creative side of themselves that can send forth love to the people who are close to them in their homes.

Kissing the snake is not an easy thing to do; and it does have hazards. It needs to be done skillfully and competently. We need to look at just what those skills and competencies are, and I intend to share these skills later in the book. But for now, let's look at the duality of love.

It goes way back. In the ancient Greek myths, there is the supposed goddess, Eros. Thanks to her, there is now the word *erotic*, which is derived from her. Look at the word. Do you think of pornography? And yet Eros is not pornography. Eros involves the skill of loving. To point out the dichotomy, the Greeks also had a brother of Hypnos, who was the false Greek god of sleep. And the brother of Hypnos was the false god, Thanatos, the supposed god of death. Many people believe that Sigmund Freud came up with this idea of a "sex instinct" and a "death instinct" from this duality of ancient Greek culture of Eros and Thanatos (Carel 2015). Life indeed presents people with choices of living and of loving, and to do so with all of who they are; with all their senses, as well as their wills, with their thought processes and with their whole hearts. To have a choice, however, they must have a skill. When driving a car, I can choose to get on the freeway or not get on the freeway. If I don't know how to drive a car, I don't have a choice at all. The lightbulb—the awareness—just won't turn on.

One of the greatest things you and I need in order to love to the fullest is to develop that skill to love. Perhaps it begins by looking inside of us and kissing the snake with somebody loving us in that process. This somebody needs to be skilled to heal the pain and the hurt that are there from living with many episodes where we were hurt deeply, because love didn't get sent forth to us when we needed it. We are often lost and in need of finding a direction.

CHAPTER 3

LOST IN OUR WORLDS

Sometimes the best way forward is to stop. There's a poem written by David Wagoner and edited by David Whyte (1996). The poem describes a young brave going to the elder in the tribe. And in that poem and in its title, the young brave asks the elder, "What do we do when we're lost in the forest?" I put a metaphor into my mind upon that line of the poem. If we are lost in the grip of frustration and anger and hurt, what do we do when we're lost in the workplace, in a relationship, or in other situations? The poem goes on to basically say that the first thing we need to do is to stop and get to know the world that we're currently in. The main thing I get out of that poem is that if we're lost, and we want to find our way back home—I'm speaking metaphorically—if lost in our pursuits of love, how do we find our ways back to love? Love of self? Love of somebody else?

This need to first stop what we're doing and to look around us when we've lost love is why I've begun writing on this topic of the world lost in a state of darkness. I want to really delve deeply into these skills I've been writing about. We need to know where we are now. If we have a new home that, as the poem says, is called "here," then we can go out from our new home and always come back to here, because we have created it to begin with. That makes sense when we're lost in the forest: to establish a base, instead of just wandering around aimlessly in the forest, hoping that maybe we'll find something familiar that will lead us back to our destinations. Maybe we are wandering off in the wrong directions all along in our society. We need to have that home first, where things are familiar, where the environment around us knows us. We can then try going out a distance to see if there is anything familiar, and come back in order to go in another direction. And if we're really far from where we want to be, we need to use that base to go far, and then to return, and then to go far again, and then to return.

Psychology provides the discipline of assertiveness training in a less-metaphorical, more-practical description on how to exit from confused darkness. We can try several different directions in order to find illumination (Bower & Bower 1991). People are trained by this method to speak up for themselves in small situations first. Maybe due to being in a crippling, psychologically abusive situation, they don't go tackle that enormous negative relationship until they find the needed skills. They try it on small things, like speaking up for their rights to not be cut off in the grocery store aisle. They learn first how to face insensitivity and inconsideration in the small things before they strike out for the big things. But once again, people need to find someone who loves them in this journey to loving more, because they feel so alone. We need more people who can help us in that. Psychology gives us assertiveness training as kind of a light in the darkness for how to proceed when we're lost. This light can shine on different avenues to find our ways back home to love and self-love.

A lot of people who are pragmatic, and even scientific, believe that the realm of love is for the poet, for the novelist, for the songwriters, for the religious, and for the pastors. They need to take it out of metaphor and make it real. Assertiveness techniques do this. Love is not for a specific few. Love is for everyone, and everyone needs to find their individual ways into the light of love.

Christian passages in the Bible describe a man who is in deep debt and goes to the lender, and the lender completely forgives the debt (Matt. 18:23–35). The person in debt had also loaned money out, and the person to whom he loaned it came to him, and there was no forgiveness in his heart whatsoever. It was as if the love of the first lender landed on nothing because the feeling, the connection, and the gratitude that needed to be experienced with that act of love, of forgiving the debt, didn't go any further than just superficial gratitude. It's as if it had been poured into a black abyss inside the person. And perhaps this person never did kiss the snake or enter into the sunlight.

Wherever we look, there is the duality of deadness and aliveness in the world! Where do I see deadness in the world? I've come more and more to realize that in every situation there's the positive and the negative, the good and the evil, the alive and the dead, and the ability to see and the inability of blindness. Matthew's depiction of forgiveness and non-forgiveness is another example.

The deadness appears in society when a preadolescent takes up a gun, gets into a car, and shoots a stranger. This stranger is killed just in order for someone to join a gang! Look at the deficit in that young killer's life. Look at the deadness. What kind of a deadness would require of somebody to take the life of another human being in order to belong to "us"? Empathy for the person killed is gone, lost!

In one movie it was said, after a person participated in his first killing, "Don't worry. It gets easier." Is that something that really needs to become easier?

Another example of deadness in society involves war. We have more and more machines flying maybe forty thousand feet above the ground, dropping bombs below, and no one is seeing the blood that is spilled. Once again, this blind deadness is probably not a choice in most cases.

I also see blindness in the grocery store, when a parent brutally yells at a child for what comes naturally to a child—reaching out and taking a can off the shelf. That child is belittled, and the parent is in darkness about it. That child in the grocery store will go through life being somewhat disconnected from his parents, somewhat dead with darkness inside. And it won't stop with the child, who will later spread the darkness to others whom he "loves," just like that person who came to me with the math-emotional problem.

The childhood teacher of my math-anxious woman was probably blind to the pain she created. She was mistreating a sensitive and caring little girl so insensitively. That math-anxious woman was in darkness concerning math for decades afterward.

An individual need not look far to see people who are in the darkness. Just look at someone being laid off at work and being told, "It's not personal." Not personal? Not *personal*? How can there not be something "personal" in any interactions between two human beings?

I once had a teacher who stood standing in front of class, talking to a blackboard, and not noticing the hands being raised. The question asked by one hand-raiser was answered with such a strong, snippy, fast comment that it didn't really provide an answer at all. There was no interaction of learning between the teacher and the student. That teacher was disconnected psychologically from the students and in turn was teaching the students to disconnect from asking questions and learning. Learning takes place when a human connection is made, and the teacher in this case appeared incapable of connecting. He might as well have been dead to his students, lost in the darkness of nonexistence.

On a broader front, there are political demands that require teachers to have more and more and more students in the classroom in order to save money. *Money?* Money is nothing but a number. It's a number in a checking account on a computer. Quite often, student class-size decisions are established on the basis of only the numbers. No consideration is given to what the ideal number is for learning to take place between a teacher and a student. Education is not the only location for this. There is also the workplace.

Sometimes managers are so focused on being efficient that they lose sight of the purpose of the company. I was once told by a car salesman that Henry Ford wanted his company to focus upon people, and then upon product, and that then the profits would naturally follow. It had to be in that order or none of them would be any good. I believe that people are meant to come first in the order of things.

Where are things dead? I think things are dead when you're driving down a road where the speed limit is sixty-five mph, and you're watching someone going seventy-five miles an hour past a patrol officer. The officer is in the dark to so many people speeding. Is there really a "speed *limit*" here? That phrase is dead if there is no limitation placed by a greater power upon the individual driving the car. That's a kind of deadness. To protect thievery in vending machines, companies have made it almost the job of a contortionist human being to get the bottle of soda out of the machine. Sometimes there's a flap that gets in the way. Why do they have a vending machine? One would think that it's to sell as many sodas as possible. So, what do they do? They create a barrier between the person giving the money and the soda itself. And it's only about numbers—how much is paid for the soda and how many sodas have been sold. In reality, there is one person meeting the needs of another person to have a soda. And to the extent that those needs of the individuals involved in a transaction are ignored is the extent to which we have blind death. Do these examples answer the question for you? Do you see ignorant death and darkness in the world around you?

We have cartoons on deadness now in the workplace, where it appears humorous that management is making decisions that totally ignore deep needs of the workers for something extremely superficial to the head of the company. And all across America people are laughing at a human condition that's very real.

"My sources tell me, Jenkins, that you've requested one lunch break and several bathroom breaks each day. I consider that a sign of weakness. You're fired."

Image by Jerry King

An old book called *The Naked Ape* said that laughter is often a form of crying, physiologically very close to crying (Morris 1967). Have you ever laughed to the point of tears? The old vaudeville shtick—a clown comes running out onto the stage and steps on a banana peel and flies into the air, and arrives on the stage with a great big thud. And the audience breaks out in tremendous laughter. Well, to the extent that we have empathy for the people we see and hear, isn't there a hurt there?

Perhaps if we kissed the snake, there would be a different kind of laughter in our lives to choose from. Perhaps we have two kinds of comedy and laughter—the insulting, harmful kind and the refreshing, wholesome-enjoyment kind. Do we have a choice between those opposites? Have we bred the wholesome comedy? Or do we feed the insulting, crass comedy in society today?

That idea of choosing what kind of humor—the crass, insensitive, laughing-at-another's hurts versus the wholesome kind of humor—is a choice that isn't always chosen. As a fact, I believe that choice only happens in rare circumstances. Choice is such a mystery, when I look at conditioning. If I do not look inside because of the hurt, well then something has squelched my ability to choose. In cases of extreme trauma, like in war, the hurt is so great that someone not only yields by not looking at the hurt inside but also by experiencing a darkness that arrives where the choice itself belongs.

A dead darkness supplants choice. In the military, hand-to-hand combat used to be called, "hand-to-hand combat." The recent term is "intimate violence." I looked up the word *intimate* on the Internet at dictionary.com and found that it involves being very close. So I can see how the military needs to have hand-to-hand combat. Why would they call it "intimate," however? Intimate also means "closely personal." I heard someone say, "Conflict is a cry for intimacy!" To translate that with the definition above, "Conflict is a cry for being closely personal." I don't want to place violence into that context! They probably just mean close combat. But words have many meanings, and when words are used indiscriminately, it contaminates all those meanings. The definition that says that intimacy is a "warm friendship," "warmth," "personal," "getting to the private nature of another person," and it is a definition of a love that emanates from a deep and private place within. If violence is attached to that, the pain can be so strong that all the lights go out and numbness predominates. And lost in a dead darkness, the person is unable to find the self that has been buried under the hurt.

So in the love experiences where people are hurt, many might just say, "That's it! I'm not going to love anymore." They have been overpowered to make that decision, but still, they made the decision. It would be hard not to decide to avoid that pain, but still, the person could choose to take it on the chin.

Now, for those who have engaged in hand-to-hand combat, that's a whole other story. For people who come back from war with post-traumatic stress disorder (PTSD), it's as if their abilities to choose in certain areas of their lives have been completely stolen from them. The inclination is to ask, "Is that part of you even in there?" The numbness is so pervasive that they might not know anymore the part of themselves that's "in there." When Leo Buscaglia (1972) equates "love" to "life," then it follows that the opposite of love is deadness, a deep and dark aloneness. Sometimes, this aloneness is chosen with awareness.

Some people steal love from themselves! How many of us have run from love? I know how hard this section of the book is to read. Remember, for a big part of my childhood I wrestled with this perspective. The dawn will arise in later chapters by first shedding light upon the darkness. For now, what about running from love?

If people run from love, they still want happiness. When people assume they can be happy without including love, they are on a fool's errand. They start pursuing wealth to buy things. Happiness won't be found by selfish pursuits.

Viktor Frankl (1965) spoke of happiness as a by-product of being lost in an endeavor, an endeavor that one loves. Selfishness seldom does this. Some people medicate or over-medicate in a futile, selfish attempt to not feel emotional pain. All kinds of various addictions are a form of being dead inside and running without direction. People try to get away from the hurt of not being able to connect with another human being. They often are only consuming pleasure from people, a pseudo-connection. These "resources" come to be seen as commodities of pleasure, things, or just objects. An object has no need to be respected. Objects have sameness. People have uniqueness. Pat Tillman was a man who bravely displayed his uniqueness and whose death was treated as only a concept.

When Pat Tillman's mother lost her grown son in combat—she lost a hero as well. The story of Pat Tillman is amazing to read in terms of love and this deadness that I talk about (O'Connor 2007). Pat Tillman became a hero because he gave up a highly lucrative career in the National Football League. He had millions of bucks at his disposal, just by playing football. But he called upon his nature and dedication to his family and to his country, and he became a hero by joining an army ranger unit.

He was sent to Afghanistan, where he died. The dehumanizing force in our society is so big that, when Pat Tillman died, the need for a hero overcame the need for the truth. He was described as running up a hill, firing at the enemy, and getting cut down by that enemy—a very heroic kind of a scene. But this selfish description of a true hero's death was not true. The military took the image of Pat Tillman away from the person he was and more toward a number or concept of acting even more heroic. Not having many heroes in this war was a military problem. They operated not from any sense of true intimacy or closeness with the spirit of Pat Tillman but were operating on a selfish front. They described a heroic action of a *hero* that never even took place.

And then when the story came out, they used a term used that's common in the military to describe a death in combat. This term is similar to "intimate violence." The *real* way he died was called "friendly fire." Now, just imagine if you're the mother of this man: After realizing that the truth about her son's death wasn't there and fighting to find that truth—and she had fought and fought and fought—to find out by being told that her hero son, her legitimate hero son, died from "friendly fire." Man! How can a killing be associated with the word *friendly*? And how does this kind of double meaning communication affect people?

It drives people into one of the most maddening experiences known in psychology. There's an old experiment with dogs. Most college students have heard of the famous Ivan Pavlov (1924) experiments where he rang a bell, blew food powder into the dog's mouth, and the dog salivated, and he kept doing that. After a while, he could ring the bell, and the dog would salivate without food. This experiment forms the basis for understanding how two conflicting messages communicated simultaneously can breed insanity.

This second Pavlovian experiment was about "experimental neurosis." Pavlov (1924) acquired a dog. He placed him in front of a piece of paper upon which he drew a perfect circle. And instead of a bell, he taught that dog to salivate strongly whenever that perfect circle appeared in front of him. After the salivating response was conditioned into the dog, he then trained the dog to stop salivating when presented with a very obvious ellipse: an elongated circle from left to right. It's not a round circle; it's flattened. So, a perfect circle: salivate. A flattened ellipse: stop salivating. The experimenter was wondering, "What would happen if someone presented a form to the dog that was halfway between that perfect circle and that ellipse?" There in front of the dog appeared two simultaneous messages. These messages were so married together that the dog was trained to salivate and to not salivate at the same time! Right there, talk about frustration. That's a good definition right there. Which does the dog choose?

But the thing to focus on is the response of that dog. The dog began barking, growling viciously, salivating at the mouth, biting anything and everything around. And if there were nothing around for the dog to bite, he would bite himself. He would also urinate. These double messages can also make humans, not just dogs, go haywire.

"Intimate violence." "Friendly fire." What are we doing to intimacy itself? What are we doing to friendship, when we let terms like this take hold, and we train people to use these terms? This is what I would speculate that Pat Tillman's mother had to psychologically deal with on top of grief. The double messaging can be viewed as serving a function for the military, however.

A vicious, mad, angry person will kill better in battle. These people come home, however, and may sometimes look at their relationships with that term "intimate violence." It's possible that some would subconsciously equate intimacy to being violent. For how many generations has that kind of pain been inflicted? Where's the choice on all that? Right? The choice was to use the term *intimate violence*. And then we blame the violent person. The violent person has a responsibility, but the violent person doesn't know what to do when presented with these double messages. Then there's no choice at all. The person has been overpowered. The person can choose and choose and choose, and if the skill isn't there, then there's no choice possible. The person is shackled by an innate response from the human organism indicating that he needs messages that are consistent and together, or else he experiences being hopelessly lost. These dichotomies aren't only in the military.

We can look at another dichotomy in our society, and that's the dichotomy between psychology and religion. Viktor Frankl, in his book *The Doctor and the Soul* (1965), also says that he's been questioned on whether to bring spirituality into—in his case—psychiatry. He was getting it from both sides: the professional psychiatrists and the people in religion. He made a very, very astute observation. He said two things: when anyone walks on the boundary between two areas, they're bound to be viewed with suspicions from both sides. And second, he said that you better know where the boundary is, if you're walking that boundary.

So he defined the boundary for psychology, psychiatry, and the mental health fields. He said that the job of religion is to save souls. He said that the job of the psychotherapist is to show people that they have one. Think of the response of the double message to that dog. Think of examples in your own life where your feelings were clashing so much into one another that you just wanted to scream in anger, and then ask yourself a question.

Where is your soul? I'm not even talking about saving that soul. Perhaps that's for a theologian. But what do those double messages do to the soul? What does that do to the power to choose? What kind of message is it to describe a person charging up a hill, killing the enemy, and dying bravely, and then we learn the person was killed by "friendly fire"? Which is it? Hero? Friendly fire? Hero? Friendly fire? I mean, which one do we choose? Who was Pat Tillman? Pat Tillman was a hero. And the love he exhibited to his country, to his sport, to his family—that needs to outshine all of this double-messaging. Are people even *capable* of going past those double-messages and seeing the man that offered so much? How much is a true inspiration from a free spirit's soul made *invisible* by everything around him? How much love is denied?

Now, what kind of a position do we place people in to choose love? It's no wonder why they look to wealth and drugs and other forms of escape from looking inside and kissing that snake.

If someone gets the courage to do that—to look inside, to look at the pain—maybe one of the first understandings we need is to realize that pain isn't always bad. Too much of anything will kill you. We don't think of water from a pristine brook up in the mountains high in some foreign, unpopulated country as being toxic. But we can drink that stream water. If we drink 150 gallons in one day, we'll be dead. So, water not only sustains life; it can be toxic to life, if there's too much.

So can we look at our pain inside? Perhaps we're even living in a society where there's so much pain that we can't even drive on a freeway in a loving manner. Maybe we're avoiding pain so much that even that degree of pain that can strengthen us and deepen our love is being squelched. Many of us are not even allowing such pain to have a chance. There's a relationship between love and pain. Do we think the universe is just here to provide power to take away all our pains and to give us wealth and everything we need? There are those who believe that. There are those who believe we're missing out on a lot, because we're not tapping into this part of the universe that's just going to give us everything we want, free of charge. All we need to do is claim it, and it's ours

(Byrne 2002). Such a belief would lead me to choose no pain at all. And then what do I lose? Pain has its place. Pain brings me to the point where I realize that I'm *not* all-powerful, that I can't just click my fingers and reality will get in line and do everything I want reality to do.

How much arrogance is there where one believes that one's will—that what one wants—can be imposed upon an environment? A lot of marriage relationships can be defined that way.

"Do it my way!"

"No, let's do it my way!"

"No, my way."

"My way should win." *Should win?*

I talked to someone once who was very deeply hurt as a young adolescent and was overpowered. After that overpowering, after that feeling of nothingness that comes from somebody trying to steal who that person is and being somewhat successful at it, this person decided, "I will never be a victim again. I am not a victim." And so much of that person's life has been lived in the form of, "I will always win. The people who oppose my winning, *they* will from now on be the victim." What kind of win is that?

Yet, there is a substantial number of highly successful people in this society who are coming from that very position. We coin terms like, "win/win," and then the "win/lose" people show up like crazy.

What the person that insists on abusing in order to win does not realize is that the *victimization* is still in control. The winner is no less a victim than the victim. People who have to win all the time don't know what it's like to get past arrogance and to experience a situation free of a need that will never be met. The need to avoid pain will never be met on this planet. Hurt is not avoidable. People are going to be hurt. And you and I are going to be hurt in this society. We won't come out of a victimized darkness of the soul by adding to that hurt by "winning"!

Now, if I have a point of view that I'm going to win every single time, well, guess what? Hurt disagrees. When I'm hurt, I haven't won. That is just as much a crazy-maker as a circle and an ellipse is to a dog in experimental neurosis. "It's incomprehensible that I'm in pain!" It's putting me at the top of reality and that reality should do my bidding. And it just ain't so. It just ain't true. Loving provides us with a healthier view of pain.

I don't know where I got this concept, but there are a couple neat metaphors about love, including that love is like a bowl. One of those metaphors stipulates that there's only one way to make your bowl large and deep, and that is to experience pain. The extent to which I reject pain, reject winning, reject relating or loving, then that is the extent to which I have a very shallow bowl, a very shallow offering of love to give someone. Now, I can't have the kind of pain that overpowers me. I need the kind of pain that I can choose to feel and feel to completion. I need to feel the whole of the pain to completion, not just parts of it.

CHAPTER 4

LOVE IS PAINFUL

There's a whole brand of psychology called Gestalt psychology that's based upon an important concept. There are many concepts, but one of the fundamental concepts is that we have "figure" and "ground" in Gestalt psychology (Barlow 1981). One psychologically forms a figure against the background of everything that is seen. The figure is to be psychologically destroyed—completed—in order to focus and create another figure. So someone looks at a lamp until done seeing it and then destroys that figure, that focus on the lamp. Attention may then be turned to the light switch, and another figure is formed against the background of that same wall that was behind the lamp. A lot of mental illness is defined in terms of being *stuck* on the figure. An individual can become stuck upon what is being focused upon. Someone might worry about the safety of a child, for instance, and think about only that over and over and over and over again. Many people wake up in the middle of the night and can't get some things out of their heads. They're stuck on the thoughts in the brain. The individual needs to finish the worry about the safety of the child. The amber caution light needs to be on, but there is a need to finish it nonetheless. Maybe there's nothing that can be done for the safety of that child, and the worry needs to be let go. How can someone let go of wanting safety for the child? And yet,

Gestalt psychology would say, "Finish it. Finish that business and move on."

It's interesting in the Pat Tillman case, there are those that say, "Let it rest. Don't push for the truth. Don't find out that he died from friendly fire." Well, you can't finish an image that has dangling issues on it.

There are others who say, "Let's make it so that Pat Tillman can be at peace. Let's get the whole story and get it out there, so that there can be peace about how he died."

Either way, form the figure and finish it. And pain can be viewed as that figure. When I have deep emotional pain, when I see something inside of me that is ugly and mean and anti-love, in a way there's a knee-jerk reaction to just not look at it. I mean, I don't want to be defined that way. It hurts my view of who I am to realize that I have this ugliness inside me. How much easier is it to run from that, or try to make it go away by drinking, taking drugs, gambling, or any number of other ways to escape?

Or how about the alternative: if it doesn't create the kind of pain of total numbness from a severe abuse that cannot be processed without help, I can focus on the pain of loving and choose the hard route of loving again. I want to focus the spotlight upon the idea that such a feeling of pain can be felt to completion. And if we develop that skill to bring self-love to where the love from the other caused so much pain, then there comes a relaxation and a freshness and a beauty that is true humility. Humility isn't losing every time to the other person. It's not putting myself below the other person all the time. Humility is like a dedication to the truth. Humility is getting to the truth, acknowledging the ugliness and the beauty. You can't have the beauty without the ugliness. We need to get past the ugliness to reach the beauty. It's bringing everything into the light!

To illustrate, put a trombone in the hand of a kid in grammar school and listen to the screechy notes day after day, week after week, month after month, and one will hear the ugliness. The beauty coming forth from that child to go through all that ugliness, and then to be able to hear that trombone in later years in synchronization with a symphony, is a wonderful thing. Look at that beauty. Look at the beauty that came from listening to the ugliness—to finishing the ugliness. It's like coming out of the darkness to see and to hear such beauty.

Through pain, I invite you to kiss the snake and to get to the beauty inside of you. Turn on the light switch. Sometimes we need an expert to do that. Sometimes it feels like we have no choice. Sometimes the pain is too early in life, maybe so early that we can't even identify it. Sometimes it can only come out in little pieces. In order to avoid the dark abyss, sometimes it's necessary to just put one foot in front of the other and move forward. A life of choosing love is a life of choosing to deal with the pain as much as we can. Choosing love is seeking truth, is seeking the beauty, and by doing so, we will be able to discover the fresh morning light of love.

I'm here to tell the world that I have a soul. I'm here to tell the world that you have a soul, that they have souls, and that we all have souls. Pat Tillman had a soul, a hero's soul, and people will only find a hero's soul in truth. People need only look at the illusion of the ugliness to get to that beauty of the man fully capable of charging up that hill, that fantasy they created to hide the pain of the truth: friendly fire. And that soul is a soul that grows with love and shrinks with indifference. People are not objects or PR concepts. People have the potential to connect with one another in a spirit of love.

Another experiment from psychology: Harlow's monkeys— is an old, old experiment. Harlow (1971) took monkeys and completely removed them from any simian contact—with their mothers or any other monkeys—no physical or caring touch. He did this in order to keep his laboratory sanitary. And what happened to those monkeys? They were completely shut down, with such a forlorn look in their eyes. Oh, if you could just see the picture of them. They're like eyes without souls, trapped with pain. They had all the food they wanted. In essence, they had all the wealth they needed. They had all the housing they needed. They had all their needs met, except the need for simian touch, and those monkeys were so abnormally devoid of being able to interact. They were deprived at such an early age that later, I imagine, they would be starving for touch and affection, and it would be almost impossible to ever give them enough. Their abilities to interact—and even to mate—with other monkeys were severely hampered. In some cases, the mothers of offspring would murder their babies. Could it be that one of the major answers to the human abortion debate lies in the early childhood treatment of the parents of our babies? Perhaps human touch in infancy is one of the answers. Human touch seems to me to be essential for love.

Love is a word we read about in psychology. Love is a word we read about in religion. It is time for psychology and religion to quit fighting each other. For example, many Christians will only refer to humanistic psychology as "secular humanism," with a derogatory tone of voice. It is so very rare to hear the words *humanistic Christianity.* Many mental health professionals attempt to restrict psychology to observable behaviors, thereby ignoring the human soul. There needs to come a time when a psychologist can widely speak to love and allow religion to be a part of that discussion.

Religion also needs to embrace and learn from psychology more. As long as there's condemnation going over that border between the two, the two disciplines are never going to learn from each other. Is it enough to awaken the human spirit and to not save it? I have just crossed the boundary with that statement. I come as a counselor trained in the field of mental health, and I ask the question that can only be answered from the other side of that boundary. Frankl's logotherapy addresses spiritual choice. I am violating Viktor Frankl's caution. I'm crossing the boundary, and I am saying, "Is it right to show another human being that they have a spirit and not even address the saving of that spirit?" To not do so is to do to humanity in the spiritual realm what Harlow did to those monkeys in the emotional realm. Psychology need not deny the love that comes from a spirit, or soul, that is saved.

John says, "God is love" (1 John 4:16). Wherever God is, so also is love. He didn't say God is like love, that part of God is love. He said *God is love.* So, when Matthew writes, "For where two or three are gathered together in my name, there am I in the midst of them," love is also in their midst (Matthew 18:20). I believe that it's time for the two disciplines of psychology and religion to come much closer together. It is time for psychology to show religion what it can do to teach the Christians, the Mohammedans, all the religions how to love even more.

Gandhi (Goodreads.com) made a statement that said, "I like your Christ, I do not like your Christians. Your Christians are so unlike your Christ." Wow, look at that. One of the greatest men for peace in the twentieth century pointing out that to be like Him, to be like Jesus, man must learn the skill to love. This concept is spiritual, as well.

"This is how all will know that you are my disciples, if you have love for one another" (John 13:35). There are those who are going to be incensed, angry, to even suggest that it's possible that there's something wrong with a Christian, that there's some kind of deficit of love with a Christian. Well, all they have to do is look at Christ's words. He said we all have to be forgiven, because we don't know what we're doing. Christians need to look at love, look at it deeply. Christians need to look at it not only theologically, philosophically, in literature—but need to look at it psychologically, as well. And psychology is just starting to uncover some of the answers, because looking inside to the pain and the hurt, there are ways that a person can look inside of that pain and hurt *with love!* If that pain and that hurt came from indifference, from a situation devoid of love, if that's the by-product of non-love, then it takes love to go in there and to change it, and that takes trust and faith.

Now, I'm still being philosophical. I'm still going to save the steps on how to practically do that for later, because there's another important step here. When I find myself in the throes of intimate violence, hand-to-hand combat psychologically—let's call it mind-to-mind violence, mind-to-mind combat, intimate violence—then I'm opening my spirit to another human being. I can get violence in return, and even violence in the name of love. Do you remember the experimentally neurotic dog (Pavlov 1927)? I was once told this double message: "I'm only hitting you because there's something wrong with you, and you need to change because you are *not good*. And I'm doing this for your own good. I'm telling you these things for your own good." The double-message here is that "I love you" and "I'm hurting you" at the same time.

Such a double message can just destroy some hearts looking to build love in their lives. All of a sudden, I went from experiencing peace and tranquility to an emotional foaming at the mouth from the double message. I wanted to just scratch somebody's eyes out—anybody's eyes. Add to this situation that such double-messaging could come at almost any time, and anyone could see why I had to always be on my guard against this dynamic, a dynamic that I didn't even understand at the time.

There is a way to bring love to this knee-jerk reaction—a way to stop the experimental neurosis, erase the pain, and come out the other side without blowing up. How often, after many of us explode in anger, just laying into somebody that we care about—how often afterward do we go, "Oh, no! What did I do? Why did I say that? Why did I think that? Why did I explode?" And we talk about "why." What a futile question. What's going on is that we have these triggers from our past experiences that immediately throw us into the grips of frustration and anger. Automatic. Lightning-fast. Before we even can realize what's happening,

35

we're screaming and shouting and figuratively trying to scratch somebody's eyes out. I hope to present the skills to stop this knee-jerk reaction before it gets triggered. There are so many junctions in life where this whole dynamic can be triggered.

How much does having knee-jerk reactions of anger describe a lot of marriages today? How much does that describe a lot of failed marriages, where love turned into experimental neurosis, or into a just totally unacceptable situation? Where the only option that could be seen would be to flee in order for one's own sense of peace and love? Fleeing isn't always bad. How much better it would be if people had a psychology-religion of what to do to come out of the throes of that knee-jerk response to anger, frustration, and all the negative emotions? Such an answer is available if people can only find it, learn the new skill, and care enough to practice that skill on a regular basis in their lives. Sometimes this whole knee-jerk scenario can get so dark that our humanity even seems to disappear.

Viktor Frankl wrote another book called *Man's Search for Meaning* (1959). In his book, he describes his experiences in the Nazi concentration camps of Dachau and Auschwitz. He describes how conditions were so bad for the prisoners there that all they had to do was give up fighting, give up the search for living, and within hours or minutes they would be dead. So deprived of food, nourishment, touch, and connection to their healthy lives from the past—like Harlow's monkeys—the dark deadness grew inside, and many chose just to die.

Society now faces suicide in youth at a rate that is unacceptable. Needs just are not being met. We can teach them the demands of Christianity. It's not too hard to look into the Bible and see what I think is an impossible demand from God, in many ways. Now, I'll also say that God can do the impossible, but He is asking for the sun not to set before we get rid of our anger (Ephesians 4:26). Remember? We wake up in the morning, and we have angry stories on the radio. We turn on the TV; we see acts of violence.

We see love without love. We see sex without true connection and bonding. We see consumption of people as objects. We are treated as an instrument for wealth for someone else at work. We get caught up in the vanity of our own lives, pursuing the desire to *not be the victim*, and to never lose, even if it means someone else loses. And we're supposed to let that anger subside before we go to sleep? You know, even if we *do*, how often does it wake us up from our unconscious minds in the middle of the night, hopelessly controlling our minds into a state of frustration?

In Ephesians 4:31, Paul says to the Ephesians, "All bitterness, fury, anger, shouting, and reviling must be removed from you ..." Do Christians actually know how to do that? Is there *anybody* who never has grudges against others? What is Paul doing here when he tells us to not lose our tempers or raise our voices when somebody crowds our space and steals something from us? And we shouldn't call each other names. How does one not call people names when it comes out of one's mouth before even having the *ability* to censor it? Paul goes on to say, "Be kind to one another, compassionate, forgiving one another as God has forgiven you in Christ." Well, now, that just sounds nice. That just sounds beautiful. That just sounds like something that *I can't do*. And Christians are taught that this is God speaking through Paul to us. Do Christians really keep anger from going on beyond the sunset? Now, neurology provides a lighted path for getting to what Paul is telling us in the scriptures. I believe people from earlier populaces knew intuitively what neuroscience is discovering objectively today—namely, how to more effectively stop their negative reactions.

As a mental health worker, as a psychotherapist, I have to say to those preachers saying to us to quit being angry as the scripture commands, "Show me how!" And as a psychotherapist, I have to say, "And can you show me how in a specific, practical, pragmatic way that's free of psychology?" I don't think so. And as a psychotherapist, I have to say to other psychotherapists that I think we have some answers to this dilemma, and it's time for us to go across that boundary with open hands and to say, "Here is how. As soon as that ugliness from inside raises its head—the ugliness of spitefulness—here is what you do ..."

Because I, as a Christian, do not believe that Jesus would have commanded us to love one another unless there was *a way* for us to love one another. You know, these words from Ephesians are just words. I need more than words. You tell me to love my enemies? I won't ask why. I'll ask, "How?"

How do I love my enemy? What do I think? What thought is so powerful that it can stop that knee-jerk reaction, when I find my fist flying through the air wanting to hit somebody, or to scratch out their eyeballs?

Now, I'm sure we can turn to another part of the Bible where it says, "Receive the Holy Spirit" (John 20:22).

"*How* do I receive the Holy Spirit?"

"Repent."

"*What* is repentance?"

Do these people who repented and gave their lives over to Christ—are they free of spitefulness? Remember what Ghandi said, "Your Christians are so unlike your Christ" (Goodreads. com). I'm not just saying the words coming out of Christian mouths. I mean the words that are in their hearts. It's one thing to shove spitefulness down. It's one thing to ignore the ugliness. It's another thing to fundamentally change one's heart in this current world. Sometimes shoving it down and denying it has very destructive consequences.

I listened to a woman tell me once that she was counseling a child in a family where law enforcement officers intervened in the violence, and that it was the professional opinion of that counselor to remove that child from that violent situation. And the law enforcement officials refused to do it, because that particular law enforcement officer *knew* that that child was in a "good family." Isn't denial wonderful? Doesn't it just make things look so much better? Isn't it so much easier to say, "No, that ugliness in that 'good' family couldn't have taken place!" Is it possible to have goodness without badness? Show me any human being alive today who meets the criterion of only being good. When we do this denial unconsciously, then we need to at least forgive ourselves.

Forgiveness. That's another big word. How do we forgive? Let me tell you something: someone doesn't start heading down that black hole of ugliness inside without going there, not only armed with love, but armed with forgiveness. You know what? Forgiveness—it's being said in psychology all over the place—forgiveness is not for the person being forgiven. It's for the person doing the forgiving. Now that's a crazy maker! "You mean, if I let this person off the hook—I mean, they hurt me. They owe me! You mean, if I just erase that debt, *I'm* the one that benefits? But they *owe* me!"

We can get religious, too, you know. Go to the Old Testament: an eye for an eye, tooth for a tooth. Well, what about that? Where is my tooth for the tooth that person extracted from me, that pain that person inflicted on me? I have a right to deliver pain where pain is given. It's in the Bible (Exodus 21:23–25)!

Then, along comes the New Testament, and the New Testament says: Always turn the other cheek (Matthew 5:38–39). Forgive one another? Love one another? Forgive the debt for me?

We need to look at that. Psychology is saying that love leads to mental health. Religion needs to infuse love even more throughout its domain, instead of just arguing that religion came up with it first. Of course, religion came up with it. Psychology is just a little over one hundred years old. Religion has a whale of a head start there—thousands of years of a head start. Who cares who came up with it? Who's the expert today? In the modern world of frustration at every corner, who knows the "how" to address that frustration? It takes a partnership. It takes a partnership between religion and psychology. Psychology has a lot of the how. The how is like driving a car. Religion provides the fuel, the gasoline—the energy to drive that car. One side is saying, "It's *my* car." The other side is saying, "But I have the fuel."

Love your enemy? To every psychologist, to every humanist who says, "Religion is the problem. More harm is done in the name of religion, and wars are fought because of religion," I ask you, "How many of those wars were due to the religion? Is this what God would want from His followers? And how many of these wars were occurring due to a lack of psychology? How many of these wars were fought because of human beings being human, with not just their religions, but with all their feelings, all their insensitivities, all their sociological problems and all their political problems?" To take just one part of the human being and to say that one part is the cause of war, I say, "How in the name of rationality can you do that?"

I have painted a pretty bleak picture of society, and I did this for a purpose. If we are going to live lives of love, we need to know just what it is that we're getting into. What I've described so far are the obstacles we face. We need to identify the obstacles, describe the challenges, until finally a solution can come forward to this very, very difficult choice we are asked by God to make about love.

We face a populace that's numbed by fear, anger, and frustration. Carl Jung taught us to kiss the snake, to embrace the weaknesses that we have inside of us, so that we can deal with them. Let's consider the hard choice presented by a crowd watching someone on a tower.

PART 2

MAKING THE
DIFFICULT DECISION

CHAPTER 5

THE TOWER OF DEAD DREAMS

It has been said for centuries that it's always the darkest before the dawn. I've often witnessed that people addicted to alcohol often have to hit bottom before they quit. There's an idea borrowed by Gestalt psychology that people have a special moment in their lives when they're ready to hear the solution to their problems, a moment where they become ready for change. It's a "moment of truth." The word for this moment is the Greek word *Kairos*. As a therapist, I often witnessed those moments in people. It's the moment of choice, a moment to choose who you are. Right here, right now! I think that ultimately this is a choice of whether to love or not, "to be or not to be." Let me share the contents of an article in the news and the thoughts about choice that brought me to Kairos.

At the age of twenty-seven, a woman was fired from her job. Her friends said that she took the firing pretty heavily. Probably for this reason, she climbed to the top of a very high tower. After she spent several minutes obviously considering a suicidal leap, a crowd of several hundred people assembled around the bottom of the tower (Mob 1973).

The woman didn't jump for quite some time. Maybe because the incident was beginning to become boring to those assembled below, someone very animatedly and humorously yelled, "Jump!"

The jeering cry was repeated by several people in the crowd. They were urging her to jump to her death. For the moment at least, they wanted her to die for their own amusement.

Eventually, the police arrived, along with some firefighters. The woman's physician was called for help. The physician and two firefighters succeeded in convincing the woman to choose her life over her death and began to help her descend the 150 feet to the ground.

When the crowd saw that the suicide attempt was coming to a close, they began booing the woman and her helpers. As soon as the rescuers came within range, members of the crowd started throwing rocks at them. The closer the woman came to reaching the ground, the more frequent and intense the rock throwing became. By the time she reached safety, the police had a mob on their hands and had to employ dogs to disperse the people.

The whole incident was not a fluke of human nature. The incident was also not a representative sample of what human nature is. Hopefully, urging a person to commit suicide is a rare, and extreme, experience in our society. Urging suicide is, however, an occurrence that occasionally takes place. Just a few days prior to the woman's attempt to take her life, an identical crowd jeered at a man to jump from that same tower.

There is little benefit in condemning people for activities of this nature. History reveals acts of much greater atrocities than these activities. Despite the condemnations that follow, atrocities still occur in our society as well as in others. There is, however, a lesson our evolution may allow us to learn.

I learn by asking myself questions and formulating answers. So let's ask some questions about this occurrence by the tower and formulate some answers to those questions. First of all, do you believe that any of the members of the crowd below that tower would have behaved in the same way if that member was the only witness to the event?

Well, it's reasonable to assume that many in the crowd were

there for the second time behaving the same way. This assumption is based on the fact that a few days earlier, a very similar event occurred at the same place. If they had felt remorse at urging a person to jump from the tower, they most likely would have avoided the second incident. Yet, there is enough evidence to know that people act differently in a crowd than they do individually. I believe that it is most likely that, if alone, any one of those three hundred people would have called for help at the time. Most people value a person's life.

So, to ask another question, why do people violate their own beliefs in a crowd? One answer is very simple. There is a type of excitement—or energy if you will—that exists when people are in a large group. There is a feeling of importance and of being a part of something bigger than what one person can do individually. This excitement, along with the safety of being anonymous and not responsible for the group's action, seems to take control of individuals.

There's another process that occurs in groups as well. Another question brings this to light. If you were happening by this crowd at this time and were to ask yourself what options or what actions were available to you, what answers would arise? One option is to join the crowd—either quietly and passively or vocally and actively. Another option is to just leave. Both of these options offer you safety but require that the value of human life be ignored.

So, what if you wish to act out the value of treasuring human life? If you were to attempt to get the crowd to stop, there would very likely be an outcry by the crowd that would drown out your words. You'd probably have rocks thrown at you, like what the police experienced. The situation would require a very intelligent and forceful personality to have any chance of success. I have not developed that level of skillfulness. Sometimes I'm not even skilled at acting out my values in safer situations. What about you? Would you have tried to save her at the risk of getting hurt yourself?

Fear often plays a large part in hooking me from taking actions I believe I want to take. But what about all those people who behave the opposite of what they may believe. Why isn't fear hooking them and holding them back? Because of the excitement within the crowd? Perhaps their lives are so devoid of real excitements that excitement becomes a most powerful motivator. Here is something that they could only witness on television, and this time it really was "live and in color," and not only that, they could get to be a part of the whole scenario. A participant. And all they have to do is follow what everyone else is doing. Psychology has studied these issues extensively.

Life in our society has been described by several authors as meaningless and devoid of feeling (Fromm 1981). Many people have been consumed by apathy, and they no longer know how to direct their lives. They're lost in the darkness of not choosing to love, and they're fearful of the light. Love provides a clarifying light in that love offers a direction to actions. So many people don't know how to create commitments that have a chance of enduring for any length of time, much less lasting a lifetime. Both the woman on the tower and the crowd below the tower are supporting evidence for this view of the human race being so bankrupt on the ability to love. *What is it like to live a life so short on meaning and worth?*

Edgar Allen Poe wrote many works about the macabre. Was he, himself, so strange that his writings would stand out so much? What process in our culture would account for so many movies being made about atrocities and supernatural evils? Perhaps the writings of Poe, apart from the genius of his expressions, were so powerful that they could awaken powerful feelings in an emotionally dead people. Perhaps the escalation of atrocities in so many motion pictures to greater and still greater cruelty is needed for a people becoming more and more insensitive to life around them. Is this what Poe experienced when he wrote the following (1849)?

A Dream within a Dream
Take this kiss upon the brow!
And, in parting from you now,
Thus much let me avow—
You are not wrong, who deem
That my days have been a dream;
Yet if hope has flown away
In a night, or in a day,
In a vision, or in none,
Is it therefore the less gone?
All that we see or seem
Is but a dream within a dream.

I stand amid the roar
Of a surf-tormented shore,
And I hold within my hand
Grains of the golden sand -
How few! Yet how they creep
Through my fingers to the deep.
While I weep—while I weep!
O God! Can I not grasp
Them with a tighter clasp?
O God! Can I not save
One from the pitiless wave?
Is all that we see or seem
But a dream within a dream?

That hope would fly away like sand in the wind, or a vision becoming more and more blurred, scares me. Furthermore, if hope does not exist, and if hope is a meaningless dream, then my fear is very real indeed. I would have to give up the hope for a happy, loving, and secure life. Yet Poe had hit on another frightening chord within me. The meanings I give to my life often slip away into oblivion, into a "pitiless wave." Can you remember a person in your life who used to give your life so much meaning and who is no longer available? Can you remember setting a direction for your life that was exciting at the time but that has faded into the realm of unattained possibility? If you are like me, you must grieve such life events, like I do. And we're not the only ones.

I knew a young man who was undergoing divorce and facing the frustrations of a direction in life becoming lost for reasons not really understood. He described an analogy that was very potent. He said that there are times when he has it all together. Life is a wonderful experience, and hope with dreams abound. New frontiers are being explored with vigor and excitement, as new skills and possibilities emerge. He said that it's like watching oneself on the television. "There it is," he said, "*The John Doe Story.* Then some SOB switches the channel on me, and I'm living my life by someone else's script." Consider the emptiness that is left after being turned off, passed over, ignored—forgotten, even, as if he never even existed.

When someone destroys a meaningful relationship with me—or one that is perceived to be meaningful—or when one of my ambitions is shattered by an aggressive person whose main motivation is to dominate me—I have very powerful, negative emotions. The hurt goes so deep inside of me that I become overwhelmed by anger and bitterness. The pain displaces the hope and leaves a very dead nothingness to my life. The experience is like having an important part of me, that says yes to who I am overridden by a world that says, "No, you're not who you are." That no—that nothingness inside of me—kills the pain and hurt like an anesthetic, medical painkiller. The deadness that others have kills a person's greatness like a television channel being changed from a great movie to a soap opera. At such times in my life, to formulate a dream seems to be the act of a fool. To pursue meaning is like a pursuit for something that does not exist. Perhaps that woman on the tower had similar beliefs.

If you've shared this feeling of hurt, and if it is a feeling which we've all shared at times, then it's no wonder that three hundred people watching that tower wished to witness the death of someone's life. If life requires love, and love can be washed away by faceless waves of misfortune, then why endure the gut-wrenching pain of love lost? Why live, if all your meanings in life slip away like grains of sand creeping between your fingers into nothingness? The fear of death is powerful indeed, if it perpetuates such a life. How do people continue against such forces?

There's a middle ground between the pain of loving through selecting meaning in life and the pain of choosing suicide. The middle ground is to adopt what I believe to be the great human illusion.

An illusion is a view of reality that one perceives as a very little part of the actual nature of the reality observed. Usually, an illusion is a view of an event, person, or object in a manner that is controlled by someone else. For example, a magician creates illusions such as sawing a woman in a box in half, and then having her emerge from the box intact. So many people go through an entire life with the illusion of not being of any worth and then acting the part of a magician to create the illusion in others that they are of great worth.

The first part of the great human illusion is that an individual does not have worth. This illusion is usually created by the view that others have. Let's now ask what views others have. Does a boss, spouse, or school teacher view someone in a manner similar to her parents? Did anyone's father view him in the same way as his mother when growing up? Does a salesman, who tries to sell a car, view the customer in the same way as a minister would? The different parts of my life often demonstrate demands upon me that are different and quite often conflicting. The hug of an important child in my life is viewed as wonderful. To hug a person at work is often taboo and would be viewed as inappropriate. So, if I am a hugging person and expected not to hug in parts of my life, aren't I being told to not be myself? The hugging part of me

49

is told that I am not of worth at work. The same could be said of all the parts of me that make up who I am. In some parts of my life, I am supported; but in all too many other parts of my life I'm expected not to be me. It's like sparkles on water. I shine in one place, and I don't get to shine in other places. Thank God for those sparkles, at least.

The second part of the great human illusion is that an individual must always appear as a person of great worth. Most people appear to me on the surface as if they are leading perfect lives free from all pain. How often do you hear someone say to you that he is leading a boring and meaningless life? Have many people that you've known, who have undergone a divorce, say to you that the pain of failure questions whether happiness will ever be found in life again?

I see many people living lives where feelings are very closely guarded or not allowed to be felt at all. This repression of feelings is the middle ground between loving and taking one's life. Let's look at how many people behave when they are in conflict with someone else. These are the times when what one person believes is right, others believe is wrong, or vice versa. The second part of the great human illusion requires people to be viewed as right all the time. Losing is unacceptable. An excellent method of being right all the time has been psychologically developed. I've defined this method as contextual redefinition.

Let's suppose that I have said that if a Republican is elected to the presidency, then a recession will not occur. Let's suppose that there is now a Republican president, and there is a severe recession. I'm approached to have the issue raised with me, because I was obviously wrong. I must create the illusion that I am always right in order to communicate that I am of great worth. I can redefine the context of my earlier statement to you and still pretend to win the argument. I may say, "You see, when I said that, the Republicans hadn't settled on a candidate. The candidate I wanted for president didn't win the nomination. He was a true

Republican. The Republican who won the presidency acts like a Democrat by not balancing the budget. This only proves my point that Democrats create recessions."

Contextual redefinition is the art of changing the meaning of a statement at a later date into another meaning by giving importance to different circumstances than were originally emphasized. The past is gone. There is only now. One cannot go into the past to verify the meanings of what I have said. I can take advantage of that fact with the use of contextual redefinition and defend my image with others, as well as my image of myself.

What do you feel like when forced to tell someone that you were wrong? I feel scared in such situations. I'm scared that others will see into the part of me that feels worthless and will then treat me as worthless. I don't think people want worthless people around them. They might also make me look foolish in situations that are important to me. Contextual redefinition can insulate me from those fears and allow me not to feel them. I can even go a step further and choose to believe the new meaning I've created. This would really protect me from any feelings of failure and low self-respect. What about these fears?

In the Old Testament, God says to Jeremiah (1:5), "Before I formed you in the womb I knew you, before you were born I dedicated you, a prophet to the nations I appointed you." So, if God knew us eons before we were born and appointed separate missions to each of us, then who are we to hold ourselves in such low self-esteems? He knew our traits and certainly had the power to tweak those traits over the millennia. Our job is to accept ourselves, our traits, as we are in full knowledge that we can't veto the goodness of those traits, unless we form an illusion that we have such veto power over God.

Put another way, let's go back in time to when various species were coming out of the oceans onto land. One member of one of those species was an ancestor to us, according to evolutionary theory. Since that time, evolution has mutated that species a countless number of times. For me to be here after such natural selections over and over again is a remarkable feat. The odds of me, or anyone else, even happening are mind-boggling. Of the hundreds of millions of sperm cells entering one's mother, only one impregnated her ovum to make each of us. And how many times has that happened over the ages? I say that if you insist on evaluating your worth, the only rational evaluation is that you are remarkable and astonishingly strong.

So, there's really no reason to label oneself as low. Only rate one's actions or behaviors. Each one of us has God-given traits. To define those traits as right and someone else's traits as wrong is to place labels on people that insulate the labeler from negative feelings. The extent to which someone convinces other people that one's labels are true is the extent to which one can gain power over one's own emotions. If everyone says that I am wrong, then it's hard to feel good about myself. How much easier is it to not adopt the great human illusions and just be myself?

CHAPTER 6

THE LABELING ILLUSION

Many religious people come from the position that humans are inherently bad. I say that this is an illusion, because many of those same religious people have a scripture that says otherwise. In Genesis, just after He created man and woman in His own image, it reads, "God looked at everything he had made, and found it very good" (Genesis 1:26–31). So the illusion is that humankind is inherently bad. This provides a religious reference for one of the most basic of humanistic beliefs. Labels of badness are used and done so incorrectly. Attribution theory in psychology consistently verifies that the situations people find themselves in have more power for determining "bad" behavior than does the personality (Miyamoto & Kitayama 2002). We really need to quit placing labels on people and start recognizing the power of situations for determining behavior.

How many great works have been lost to the human race due to the form of labeling that is known as discrimination? Discrimination is based upon labeling. How many women in history never had the opportunity to become successful writers, never had the opportunity to be outstanding mathematicians, and never got to become architects of wonderful buildings? The deck was always being stacked against them simply because of the label, "woman!" What might we accomplish if all of this talent, which is going numb due to pain that's so great, could be liberated and could be cultivated with love?

Have you ever been called stupid? Clumsy? An idiot? Have you ever been referred to with an obscene word? Or as being worthless? When these descriptions get to me inside, I feel defeated, numb, and vindictive. I sense that someone else has an evil power over me, and I don't like it. That power to label another person, object, or event may indeed be one of the strongest of psychological powers that most people possess. Those who seek popularity know the power of labeling. Power is often the motivation for seeking popularity. How does this work?

Labels evoke feelings in people. How do you feel about the following words—death, loser, alcoholic, cancer, concentration camp? Take each word, dwell on each one for a moment, and then check your feelings. The power of a label need not be negative. Let's dwell instead on words like exuberance, vibrant, winner, healthy, and party. Now check your feelings.

Have you ever been called intelligent? Athletic? Wise? When these descriptions are applied to me and reach into my inside; then I feel successful, competent, and appreciative. What is often overlooked, however, is that someone being positive is also exercising power over me with adjectives. Since I like these descriptions of me, that power doesn't usually feel evil. The descriptions feel beneficial.

Whether the labels from others are positive or negative, and I receive them into myself, I am being manipulated to some degree. By receiving them, I either knowingly or unknowingly allow my feelings—my self—to be moved in some direction.

I can hurt or be hurt by labels. I can heal or be healed by labels. I can become discouraged or inspired. There is another quality about labels. They often take on the sense of permanency. It's hard to think of a happy person as unhappy. It's hard to think of a liar as telling the truth, as if one event of lying is indicative of a permanent and pervasive pattern.

For a moment, let's look at any random object of existence. Does that object—whatever it might be—remain the same, or does it constantly change? I believe that all objects change. The atoms that make up any object are always moving. If I could measure temperature to a billionth of a degree, I would see the temperature of any object gyrating constantly. If I could connect someone to an instrument that could very sensitively measure all the feelings that the person was experiencing and how potent those feelings were, I would see many feelings rising and falling all the time. Colors vary with ever-changing intensities of light and differing filters through which that light passes.

In a sense, everything around you and me is now ever changing in every moment. What do you hear right now? Whatever it is, isn't it changing in volume and in tone? Don't you hear something different now from what you heard an instant ago? Labels become dangerous to my well-being when I give them the illusory power of permanency, because I can miss out on so many possibilities never seen. God gave us an infinite and flexible world of change to entertain our senses. We then try to impose our limitations on that wondrous creation through the use of labels. Let's see how changes and labeling relate to the great human illusion.

Labels perpetuate the great human illusion. Defining myself as thoroughly competent, or even incompetent, is to freeze my ability to change and grow. If I'm competent, then I must avoid the new area where I'm not skilled. These new areas may threaten me with beliefs of incompetence when I fail. Thus, I'm depriving myself of new learnings. And what about others?

To create permanent labels in my mind about the people and events in my life is to give me a sense of security and safety in life. I tell myself sentences like, "He screamed at me just because he's that way. He's a frustrated person." This simple label, that he's a frustrated person, easily absolves me of any guilt. Even if I'm not a casual party to his screaming, the label makes it easier for me not to become involved in helping him to overcome his screaming.

This appears safe to me, because involvement with him may lead to more screaming by him, which might be directed toward me.

To be honest, I'm less secure by using permanent labels. By absolving guilt or avoiding other unpleasant feelings by using labels, I'm avoiding action to deal with my challenges in life. By avoiding action, I'm not learning what actions succeed and what actions fail in the circumstances of life. I'm, therefore, stopping my development as a person.

In reality, people and events are always changing. "Frustrated people" are more or less frustrated in different circumstances and at different times than what is thought about them. They can also be calm for long periods of time. They cannot be "frustrated people." Who a person is, who I am, and who you are is not so easily defined.

Labels I place upon others are usually whatever feelings, thoughts, or behaviors that I—or they—are feeling, thinking, or doing. Sometimes those labels tell more about what I am experiencing, than what they're experiencing. For example, if I don't understand their ideas, then I label them as "stupid." In this case, the label merely demonstrates that I understand different concepts than they.

A simple rearrangement of habits of thinking and communicating could catalyze my personal growth. If I replaced the label of "stupid" with the thought, "I don't understand," then I can formulate questions that may lead to me learning something new. The best part of this approach to my thinking habits is that one party need not be smarter than the other. I need not enter into that great illusion. The "famous genius," R. Buckminster Fuller, may have said it best in describing himself, "I live on Earth at present, and I don't know what I am. I know that I am not a category. I am not a thing—a noun. I seem to be a verb, an evolutionary process—an integral function of Universe" (Seiden 2013).

If someone doesn't use permanent labels, then how can

someone form a meaning to life? If permanent labels create illusions, because everything and everyone is constantly changing, then how can someone deal with all of life's events and people? It's beginning to appear that living a life in such a way as avoiding illusions isn't very easy, or is it?

First of all, living a life in such a way as embracing illusions is even less easy. To avoid the growth of acting and experiencing the ever-elusive world around us is to enter into the false security that we don't need to develop better and better skills of dealing with life. The day will come when those new and better skills—which were never developed—will cost us dearly. Your illusions may cost you a happy marriage, a fulfilling friendship, or advancement in your work. In essence, the only true safety is the ability to navigate danger in such a way as to create opportunity in the midst of crisis. An elusive world requires elusive living (Fromm 1994).

What do I mean by elusive living? Obviously, I don't mean escaping the demands of life. Elusion assumes the ability to move and change. Elusive living means moving with your ever-moving and ever-changing world. It means escaping skillfully from the dangers of a world that seem to be leading toward making everyone the same.

Rachel Carson (1998) has written, "The edge of the sea remains an elusive and indefinable boundary." I am incapable of permanently establishing just where the edge of the sea is. I am equally incapable of permanently establishing just where I am with my life. That does not mean, however, that I cannot find the edge of the sea; nor that I cannot find where I am with my life. Just because the meanings of my life are elusive doesn't mean that my life is without meanings. This is where Poe's poem about dreams goes so insufferably awry. To know the meanings of living requires an understanding of meaning itself.

To make a choice to resist the crowd and to not engage in labeling is a hard choice. But it is important to realize that it's a choice that God wants us to make. In Revelation 3:16 He says,

"Since you are neither hot nor cold, but only lukewarm, I will spit you out of my mouth." Perhaps He's asking us to take a stand. The stand to be taken involves a choice between two options. We can pursue a life of loving ourselves and others or pursue a life of supporting our illusions.

We face a populace that's numb. Is that what He meant by "lukewarm"—somebody who is captured in the grip of fear and unable to choose otherwise? Perhaps so. We know from modern psychology that some psychological pain is so deep that a choice to be lukewarm hasn't been made, so hopefully God will forgive those. But how many of us, when faced with a choice between life's insanities and a path of love, actually choose to remain lukewarm because of the probably-false belief that such is the way to play it safe? So many of us prefer to live in twilight when we could be baking in the warm brilliance of sunlight, if we could only learn a simple skill of loving ourselves and others!

If we're going to come out of that, we need to adhere to what the mystic poet Rumi says (Barks 2003). He says that love is the cure, that your pain will keep giving birth to more pain. The more that we ignore love, the more that pain gives birth to more and more pain. It's hard to think of a life of love as an easy life. But I think many of us have gotten to the bottom of the barrel, or we have learned that not to choose love is even worse. But we have forgotten the ancient knowledge of just how to love, how to have love be a cure from inside of us.

Rudyard Kipling is another famous poet, who wrote a poem called "If." And he starts his poem by saying, "If you can keep your head when all about you are losing theirs and blaming it on you ..." Think about that. Can we keep our heads, when all about us are losing theirs and blaming it on us with destructive labels? This is where the frustration is coming from. And yet, Kipling goes on to say that if we do keep our head in the face of all the different life challenges, we will find ourselves in a mature status later on. He says, "Then, you will be a man, my son." We need to keeps our heads when everybody else seems to be losing their heads. Understanding the power of choice in regard to the meanings we create can assist us to "keep our heads."

Victor Frankl (1969) says that we must solve what he calls an existential neurosis. In his book *The Will to Meaning*, he gives two laws of dimensional ontology, which require some visualization in order to understand. So, imagine a perfectly square room, a perfect cube. And somehow, miraculously, in that room, right in the very center, we have suspended in midair a ball, a cylinder, and a cone. This room has two lights. One light is on the wall, straight across from the three suspended objects. The other light is on the ceiling, directly above the three objects. If someone turns on the light from the wall, the light hits the cone, the cylinder, and the ball, projecting three shadows on the opposing wall. Those shadows would be a triangle, a rectangle, and a circle—which is no surprise. If, however, someone turns the light on directly above the three objects, we will see on the floor three circles.

And the point of this visualization is that we have the power to extract different meanings from exactly the same situation—or the same objects—depending on how we look at them. Those three objects can be viewed differently. When we see a cone, a cylinder, and a ball, our vision is accurate. But when we look at the three circles on the floor, those three circles are also accurate. It's our illusion of the permanence behind our labels that is inaccurate.

We have a power of choice. We have a choice in life as to what meaning we are going to give to the various situations we find ourselves in. This is a very important concept for love— and for life—because whenever we're in any given situation, we can choose, if we've developed the skill, to see either good or bad in that situation. What's more, we are perhaps unknowingly choosing how to feel, or whether to keep our heads about us. Keep the spotlight on this, that we have the power to choose our meanings in situations. If we look at life this way, as a choosing of meanings in every moment, we'll find a powerful, powerful resource for loving.

Ever since I was an adolescent, I've thought, *I want to get off of this planet.* I didn't like what I saw in the world. I saw the world as a place without love—a place of hurting people. As an adolescent, I even expressed this view to my mother, which was pretty unloving in and of itself. My mother wisely and immediately informed me that if I was right about that, then it was up to me to create some love. So, there I was trying to get people to change—to become more caring. I must say that such an orientation of myself to the world created an enormous amount of bitterness in me. I was missing an important fact about love!

I think that my mistake was that I was looking at the evil, instead of the good. Quite often an evil circumstance gives birth to a situation where somebody who chooses love can send that love to another person. One thought that comes to mind is a grenade that arrives in the middle of a platoon, and one of the soldiers chooses to immediately jump to his certain death onto that grenade in order to save the lives of the other troops in the platoon. What we need to realize is that if that evil of throwing that grenade had never arrived into the middle of that platoon, then the beauty—the choice to love—never would have taken place. The ugliness gives birth to beauty. Evil provides an opportunity to do good. Perhaps by bitterly seeing so much evil, I missed out on opportunities to peacefully see so much more good—so much more love in the world. But our perceptions require a choice. It requires a choice that is not easy to make, especially without an emotional skill that so many of us are lacking.

We still need the long-forgotten knowledge of the ancients in order to figure out how to start making choices like that. How do we live in a state of love? When life presents us with one of the frustrating, fearful situations that it is sure to present to us, how do we empower the choice to love? Well, it entails two things. It entails the power of the heart and the power of the mind.

First, let's look at the power of the mind. Psychology gives us the idea of affirmations. Psychologists, particularly Albert Ellis (1956), says that we have lightning-fast beliefs that are often automatic and negative. These create most of our psychological difficulties. We're not so much bothered by what happens to us as we're bothered by what we view as happening to us. So, he puts forth the idea that we need to change these illogical thought patterns that we have into rational ones. We need to change the bad thoughts we're having into good thoughts.

Now, to do that, we need to identify what those lightning-fast beliefs are. Well, that shouldn't be so hard. Psychology has discovered that in the English language we have many more negative-emotion words than we do positive-emotion words (Fredrickson 1998). We're spending most of our time thinking negative words. And if Albert Ellis is correct, we're thinking those negative words with lightning-fast effectiveness.

Let's say that we find ourselves in a situation that's frustrating—for example, being at the tower, when that woman was standing, ready to jump. Remember, hundreds of people were chanting, "Jump, jump, jump." We can immediately say, "I'm getting out of here. This is too dangerous for me." That's not a hard thought to identify. How do we turn that around? How do we take that weak, bad thought and turn it around into a strong, positive thought?

Believe the opposite of what we're usually believing. We need to practice a thought pattern that says, "I will take a risk for good, rather than flee in fear." According to Ellis, if we can repeat that belief to ourselves over and over and over again enough times, we will replace that weak belief with a strong belief. The positive belief that we can repeat is called an affirmation. We affirm what we choose our minds to think.

When a person creates affirmations, there are certain words that need to be avoided. Affirmations are words that we say to ourselves to empower ourselves. Words like, "I am being strong," can be repeated over and over again until the person reaches the point of a belief. Affirmations have traps. And those traps are using words like: *no, not, never, always, try, will,* and *can.* So instead of saying, "I'm not going to be weak" over and over again, the need is to say, "I'm being strong." Instead of saying, "I'm never going to be weak" or "I'm always going to be strong," the need is to start saying to oneself, "I'm getting stronger and stronger and stronger." Action-positive words are needed where the brain can accept the choice ability that we all have inside of our brains to choose good over evil, to choose strength over weakness. Finally, there is the need to believe our affirmations in the present tense. The brain knows unconsciously that the future is unknown. So, any affirmations in the future tense lack power and conviction. Be strong now by choosing now to be strong.

People are programmed with these negative beliefs, I believe, from original sin. In the garden of Eden, when Adam ate the forbidden apple, he got the "knowledge of good and evil" (Genesis 2:17). The first thing he turned to was that he was immorally naked. The first thought he had was negative. He had been living in a paradise, and all of a sudden the knowledge of evil, the knowledge of the negative, was upon him. So naturally, he focused on that. Just think what could have happened if he had the skill and used the skill to choose the positive belief to grow and to nurture.

People have been focusing on negative messages for eons and eons. They have been labeling people. People have been delivering double messages to other people and also blaming other people. And most of us have experienced all of these ourselves. The need is to reprogram those labels, those double messages, and those blaming ways of thinking into more positive, strong kinds of thinking—positive words.

At the end of every day, perhaps, you and I need to review the day we just had. And maybe, just in our imagination, we should review what we could have done in those situations when we were weak—redo them in our fantasy. We can ask ourselves how we wish we had responded. We can also ask how we could have responded in a psychologically healthy and/or Christian way to those frustrations. Then we can affirm to move in a Christian direction next time we're presented with such a choice. The more we practice a positive and healthy set of ideas in our minds, the more likely we are to respond positively in the future.

We need to clear out the garbage each day, so we can face the next day with more vibrant energy. We need to be empowered, however, from a heart of love and from feelings of love.

Let's explore these ideas of the laws of dimensional ontology, affirmations, positive, and negative thinking with an example. Let's say I'm a parent of a little boy named Johnny. Let's say Johnny is crawling around—as children do—and all of a sudden he notices the plug in the wall, and he starts crawling over toward that plug. Let's say, to make things worse, that he had his hand in his mouth before he began crawling. He gets close to the plug, and he starts reaching for the plug. Now, I, as his parent, can get a meaning from that, that this is a bad, terrible situation for my son. That interpretation would be one of the many meanings—pointed out by the laws of dimensional ontology—in that I see danger from that particular situation that Johnny is in. And so I do what every other parent on the planet would probably do. I yell at him, "No! Stop! Don't you ever do that again! You will hurt yourself! It can even *kill* you!" Now, what have I done there? Let's say I go a step further, and I say, "Bad boy! You're a bad boy!" I can think of only a few parents who would handle that situation much differently. But let's look at how the parent is handling the situation. Number one, it is a situation based upon fear, rather than based upon love. Number two, the language that's being used, "*No!* Do *not* ever do that again! You *will* hurt yourself. You *can* die." Those are the words that I gave for not using in an affirmation. Those are the words that need to be subtracted from the communication to Johnny. Now, I also do not really want to win my argument with Johnny, that he is a bad boy. Why do I not want to win the argument? Because if Johnny believes me, and he believes that he's a bad boy, then what's he going to do? When I'm not around, he's going to crawl over and stick his wet finger into that plug, because that's what bad boys do.

In addition to winning the argument with Johnny, there's an unconscious part of us that realizes that "never" and "always" are situations that are very, very rare. People usually think those words when they're wrong. Furthermore, when someone uses the word "will," that person is talking about the future. And nobody can see the future. And when I say that "can" kill you, it leaves open the possibility that it won't kill you. Those words—*no, not, never, always, try, will,* and *can*—probably create more problems than solutions.

So, how could I have approached Johnny? Viewing the situation as a situation of love, I could have said, "Johnny, stop. You see that plug? Touching that plug really hurts little boys! It gives a very, very big owie!" Do you remember when you touched the stove? Do you wish that you had touched something besides that stove? Well, if you knew how big an owie comes from that plug, I think that you would want something besides touching the plug right now."

What have I done? I have respected Johnny's ability to choose. Where else in this society is our ability to choose what we do "respected"? And yet, choice is at the essence of love. Johnny may choose to hurt himself or not hurt himself. Which do you think he'll choose? But if I label Johnny as bad, if I use that label, if I blame him, then I'm actually contributing to the creation of the very thing that I hope to eliminate.

Another expression of these concepts comes when looking at something that's boring. Instead of seeing it as boring, why not create a different reaction in our minds and feelings about it? The situation need not be viewed as dictating to us how to react. For example, little Johnny crawling over to the plug can be seen as a fascinating opportunity to love Johnny and to support his ability to choose. We need to look at the boring and perceive a fascinating opportunity to respond creatively. And even after perceiving what's fascinating, we need not stop there. Using our God-given gift of choosing, we can look for something even more creative and fascinating than the first option discovered.

It's good advice to go through life looking for more and more answers. This way an individual can put oneself into positions of most potential. Reality cannot be masterfully controlled to always do someone's bidding. A person cannot make what happens go away or change. Someone can exert ability to choose how one's going to position oneself against situations that might be harmful. A person can choose to put oneself into positions of loving other people instead of in positions of hurting other people—to use tentative, flexible, and positive labels for situations.

If I came upon that crowd at the tower, screaming, "Jump!" to that woman at the top of the tower, I would be very ill-prepared to stand in front of that crowd and to talk them out of that behavior. They were throwing rocks at the police who were trying to save the woman. How do I approach a crowd of angry people and love? Well, I need to have already found how to love in smaller situations. And I need to lead a life of looking for opportunities to love people in small ways, and then in slightly bigger ways, and then in slightly bigger and bigger ways—developing my skills of loving. Perhaps then I could get to the point where I could stand in front of that crowd by the tower with eloquent verbal skills and get them to think about what they're doing as individuals. Instead of that crowd mentality to pursue the excitement of violence, those individuals could activate the choice to love.

Krumboltz and Levin (2004) call this "happenstance." We put ourselves in positions where the odds of love taking place are greater than if we take some other action. If we are always looking for another right answer, another bigger, better, more powerful way to love somebody, then eventually happenstance is going to come along and tap us on the shoulder, and we're going to be able to deliver love in very high dosages.

The Gelatts (2004) say that we need to approach our lives with "positive uncertainty." We need to go forward in life, living with a positive view, a positive belief, a trust in God that we're going to have the opportunity to love at whatever ability that we have to love. Our searchlights need to be on in order to avoid the reefs and to capitalize on the deep waters. When we see love, we'll be able to recognize it and pursue it. But it takes positivity in the face of uncertainty.

CHAPTER 7

A WALK OF CHOOSING LOVE

These ideas remind me of my golf coach. My golf coach was teaching me how to change my swing, so I could be a better golfer. And after he trained me in this new swing, he said, "Now we have to work on you psychologically."

I said, "Wait a second. I'm trained in psychology. I know how to handle the psychological aspects of the game."

The coach said, "Well, let's look at that for a second. Let's see if you have it down. Every golfer has a golf hole that they absolutely hate. Do you have such a hole?"

And I thought of a hole at a golf course that I really hated. So I said, "Yes."

And he says, "Describe the hole for me."

I said, "Well, you're standing on the tee, and right in front of the tee is a lake—spanning the whole fairway from left to right." A tee is where you hit the ball for the first shot of the hole. "You go down this fairway—this narrow fairway with tall pine trees on both sides—and it's about a four hundred sixty-five–yard hole to the green, and that green is very challenging, because it has a lot of undulating hills on it."

He said, "When you're standing on that tee, ready to take your first shot, what do you say inside your head?"

I puffed up my chest and very proudly proclaimed, "I say to myself, 'I'm not going to hit the ball into the lake.'"

The coach said, "John, that's where you're making your mistake."

I said, "What? What mistake?"

He said, "Where's your focus?"

"On the lake. I don't want to hit it in the lake"

Remember those words—*no, not, never, always, try, will,* and *can*? "I will *try* to *not* hit it into the lake."

"Where's your focus?" he asks again.

"My focus is on the lake," I repeat.

"That's your problem. How often do you hit the ball into that lake?"

And I said, "More times than I hope to remember. That lake seems to get more balls than any other lake."

He said, "How often do you hit the ball where that lake is when you're on other holes that don't have a lake?"

I said, "Hardly ever."

He said, "Instead of saying, 'Do not hit the ball in the lake,' start saying to yourself, 'Hit the ball onto the green fairway.'"

I thought, *Come on. That simple, little change of focus is going to change my whole result on that hole?* Well, guess what? I have never hit a golf ball into that lake since he taught me how not to. Furthermore, I haven't hit the ball into the pine trees anywhere near as often as I have in the past. The point: Focus on what's positive. Focusing on the safety, instead of the danger is an important aspect of creating love in our lives, as well. Let's look at this again in yet another way.

Let's imagine that I'm walking through a forest, and I come to a small, open meadow. And let's say there's a cattle path winding through that meadow. That path of dirt is about two-and-a-half-feet wide. I have no problem walking on that path from the woods, through the meadow, to the other side of the meadow where the trees begin again. I could even run on that path and not get off the path even once. But now let's say instead of grass on either side of that path, I am on a two-and-a-half-foot-wide path with a two hundred–foot cliff on one side, and a two hundred–foot cliff on the other side. I don't know about you, but I am going to be crawling on that path. What's the difference?

The only difference between those two paths is that there's danger on the second path. In the first example, going through the meadow, it's very simple for me to keep my focus on the path and to keep myself on that path. In the second example, because there's such danger, I need to look at that danger. At least, that's the false belief I'm under. What I really need to do is keep my eye on the path. How often are we in situations where there's danger—like our son putting his finger into a plug—and instead of looking at the solution to the problem, we look at the danger? We look at the boring, instead of the fascinating. When we find an answer, we need to look for another, better one. We need to look at the opportunity to love in the bad situations coming our way.

Let's look at it through the eyes of the apostles, two thousand years ago. How would you feel if your God died—actually died? That was the experience of Peter, John, and all the apostles. The person who had taught them what love was, taught them the power of choice—if you remain faithful—imagine the darkness of their souls upon His crucifixion. Talk about fear, frustration, and anger. They must have been experiencing that fully—especially the fear in that environment, where choice was something punishable by torture and death.

Three people—Mary of Magdala, Peter, and John—went to the sepulcher where Jesus was buried, and what did they find (John 20:1–10)? They found nothing to be afraid of. What they found was a miracle, a miracle of Christ who'd risen from the dead. Certainly, under the circumstances of witnessing God dying, a person would have little chance believing that love was happening. And yet, when someone looks at Jesus, forgiving all of us for our original sins, there on the cross after all that suffering and on the brink of death—it took all of that evil that was dumped on him, for him to show the power of love to the people of this planet. Wherever there is evil, there is also good. And it's a question of having a choice of what to look at. I'm not just talking about a silver lining. I'm talking about a choice to perceive that, even in the face of evil, we have the choice to love, and to dwell in love, in the face of all of that. A person just needs to learn the loving skill and choose to practice it regularly. It turns out that such a skill is fairly easy when it is practiced regularly.

And when the resurrected Christ did come, the apostles were fearful in a room, praying. And what was the first thing Christ said to them? "Peace be with you" (John 20:19). How could they just have peace within, unless the ancients understood how to change their fear into peace? Now, certainly, the arrival of Christ would bring a lot of positive feeling, but still, "Peace be with you"?

President Abraham Lincoln (Goodreads.com) is attributed to once saying that people "are about as happy as they make up their minds to be." But once again, you don't make up your mind to be happy unless you have the skill, the ancient skill. It takes a power within us that is stronger than the brain in order to change the brain.

We can always choose from alternatives. We can choose to turn left or to turn right. We can choose to join the crowd beneath that tower and yell, "Jump!" to the woman on the tower, or to face the crowd, or to leave, or to climb the tower to try to help the young lady. We always have choices.

But the choice to be happy—how do we choose to be happy? We can choose to confront the crowd, but what's going to happen to us? We cannot choose to confront the crowd and to have an outcome that we select. The crowd is there and will most likely stone us, unless we have tremendous oratory skills. But we do have the choice on how to posture ourselves in the face of that evil. And after the crowd dissipates, who gets the attention? The person who stared them down—the person who opposed them.

Just like the newspaper article that I read about the tower, I also read an article about a shunned hero, who got involved in New York City (UPI, 1967). He witnessed a person attacking another person. And what did he do? He got involved. He went over and tried to fight the attacker of the victim, and as a result, he himself had knife wounds to his body. The intended victim, by the way, ran away, leaving him alone. And so, Curtis Stokes entered the news nationally from his hospital bed in Beth Israel Hospital. He said that although he was black, helping a person who is white, he was no Uncle Tom. And as a matter of fact, he had gotten involved in muggings several times prior to this story. And his friends were calling him Uncle Tom. He said that all he did was what anybody else would do.

Not true, not true. This was a rare human being. He could choose his response to the evil, but he could not choose the outcome. The crowd, his friends, turned against him, and he fled. He ran off to Chicago. And he couldn't live with himself there, because he had run away. That was not strength; that was weakness. Stokes returned, got involved one more time, and wound up with knife wounds, and he said he would do it again, because when he was in the Marine Corps, he learned that people are to help each other.

What a marvelous story of love. And when we juxtaposition the story of the tower with the actions of Curtis Stokes, who stands out—the crowd or Curtis Stokes? If Curtis Stokes had died at the hands of that mugger, somebody would have died—a giant somebody who commanded the highest of respect!

So many of us are afraid to look inside of ourselves, for fear we'll find nobody there. If Curtis Stokes had died in New York that day, somebody would have died, somebody capable of making choices for love in the face of evil, somebody who could look inside of himself and see a capacity to love all people, regardless of their color, regardless of who would oppose them. Unless you and I dig down deep inside of ourselves and make the choice ahead of time—a choice for love in any and all situations—only then will we know what to do when we are faced with that situation. Only then can we use the knowledge of the ancients that I'm going to provide—to wash away the fear and to allow us to choose hope and love instead, to choose that peace be really within us.

We can choose the alternative of how to respond to evil. The outcome needs to be left in God's hands. Victor Frankl (1959) once again talks about the responsibility to choose in every moment of life. Can you imagine that? How often do you and I exercise our abilities to make a choice? Frankl says in his book *Man's Search for Meaning* that at any given moment, we are capable of thousands and thousands of different actions. Right now you can put down the book; you can stand on one leg; you can put a pen in your ear; you can blow your nose. Yes, the options can go on for nearly forever. At any given moment, there are a near-infinite number of possibilities that we can choose.

A lot of times we sit there, and we look at the possibilities, like getting involved in love, and we don't know what the outcome will be. And we stand there, indecisive, not using our ability to choose. So many of us go through life lukewarm, never choosing one way or the other, never looking for the remarkable option of how to love in a given situation. All it takes is for us to start choosing.

You might ask me, "What's a choice?" My answer is that I have no idea. To me, a choice is a mystery. If I could get you to start making more choices in your life, I would be the next Sigmund Freud. I don't know how to do it. I do know that many of us have to put our fears, our frustrations, and our angers aside in order to make good choices. Psychology has even shown that to us in brain monitors (Van der Kolk & Saporta 1991). When someone is in the state of frustration, thinking becomes confused. The decision center, judgment, becomes less efficient than when we are in states of caring and of loving. We need to be in that peaceful state—"Peace be with you" state—that Christ wants us to be in.

So many people face this near-infinite number of choices

available in every second. They're afraid to choose one, maybe because of all the other ones they would lose out on. And so they stay there, lukewarm, indecisive, and choose to not choose. And the ability to choose starts atrophying, starts shrinking. *Our ability to decide whether to love or to not love declines as we become more and more lukewarm.*

Frankl (1969) says that there is a responsibility at any given moment to create meaning in life. Remember the ball, the cylinder, and the cone? You can look at many different situations and extract just one meaning. What I'm saying is, the meaning to extract from every moment in our lives is the meaning of love. Put the biggest spotlight that you can on that thought: Choose often and choose only love! We need to choose and choose and choose only love. We need to make that choice as constant as our breathing. How do we love ourselves and our fellow man? That's the issue.

Once again, Rumi (Barks 2003) says that the heart is the source of that love, not the brain. Remember, the brain has invented many more negative-emotion words than positive-emotion words. There is a strong need for the power of the heart to bring the mind into order, so that a person can start deciding and choosing love over the evil that permeates the world. How would a Christian know that such a power resides in the heart?

Psalm 27:3 says, "Though an army encamp against me, my heart does not fear." Can you imagine an army, a whole army, surrounding you, and you standing there without fear? Furthermore, before he passed away, Leo Buscaglia (1972), wrote the book, *Love*—he has a copyright on the word "love"—and he describes love fully. But I once heard in one of his talks the statement that basically said something like this: "You can smell like you've never smelled before; you can taste like you've never tasted before; you can touch and feel like you've never touched and felt before; you can hear like you've never heard before; you can see like you've never seen before; you can *be* like you've never been before." That's what I want. I want to be making choices every moment, to pay attention to the world around me, looking for love, looking at the options for me to create love. I've been there, where Leo Buscaglia mentions. I have heard and touched and seen through the eyes of love, and it's a remarkable, wonderful, beautiful way to live. Peace be with you.

The ultimate choice you and I all have is to be true to our hearts, or to choose to spend our time calculating how to remain safe. We can choose our hearts; we can choose our calculating minds; or we can choose that numbness, that kind of nobody-existence inside of us. What choice do you want to make? Do you want to choose good or evil?

Or do you choose a third choice—not choosing? I don't want to be spit out of God's mouth. Two of the three choices—evil and not choosing—result in walking alone without God. Shall a psychology teacher talk about saving a person's soul? Yes. I want to be with God in this and in the next life. But I think that choice between good and evil is seldom made. So many people go lukewarm.

The hurtful route of love requires courage. Courage is a virtue. It's a virtue of trust in God. Even not including religious considerations here, how do you want to die? Do you want to die jumping from a 150-foot tower? Or would you choose to die like Curtis Stokes? And when someone looks at a life of depression—depression dependent on losing a job, for instance—courage is needed. In the case of love emanating from the heart of Curtis Stokes, the love was for a person who never even asked for it. If Stokes had died, I tend to think he would have died with a sense of excitement and joy that he was capable of such action. Strength comes from dealing with the pain of loving. The pain is hard, but eventually, if a person learns how to deal with the pain of loving, it is so much easier than being unskilled and living with the psychological pain of not choosing love. And by not choosing—someone lets the world send oneself wherever the world will.

I believe I see so many people being different people in different situations. I think that these people don't know how to have a persona with a single value that centers them on who they are to be in different situations. This is what it takes to be a person of love. So many people are one person to their bosses, another person to their spouses, another person to their children, another person to their friends, and yet another person athletically—whatever the situation calls for. So many are choosing to be whatever that situation is calling for. Who are they, if they are so many different people?

Let's say that someone plans to go to a picnic, and all of a sudden it starts raining. And of course, the rain is unwanted. Perhaps there is the illusion of demanding that reality provide a day full of sunshine. Sitting there looking at the rain, one gets madder and madder and madder, insisting that the rain go away, and that the sun come out so that there can be a picnic. An individual cannot impose one's will upon the world. One can only choose how one's going to act upon that world. Either demand from the universe to get what one wants, or choose the beauty of love. Choose to love the rain. When someone chooses to love the rain, then the pressure, the frustration, and the anger just dissolve—provided one brings to the heart the feeling of love, which I fully intend to provide the means for you to do. There is another important choice to make first.

There is a classic experiment by a psychologist named Walter Michel (1970), where he would give four-year-old children one marshmallow and tell the children that, if they wanted to, they could eat it now. If, however, they waited until he came back into the room in a little while, they could have two marshmallows instead of one. If a person looks at the video of these poor children, they would do everything but eat the marshmallow. Some children would eat the marshmallow immediately. As a matter of fact, most of them would. The ones that waited—they would be smelling the marshmallow, picking it up, putting it down, putting it into their mouths, taking it out of their mouths, maybe taking a tiny, little bite, but not eating much of it. I view this experiment not so much in the terms of the psychological term of delayed gratification; I see the children who wait for the second marshmallow as making their decisions moment by moment, like Frankl said.

I want to eat that marshmallow. No, I'm going to wait. I want to eat that marshmallow. No, I'm just going to smell it—that's all, just smell it. But I'm not going to eat it. How many times did those children have to choose not to eat that marshmallow? And you know what? In the follow-up study, when those four-year-olds turned eighteen and were taking the college board exams, the ones who waited for two marshmallows scored 250 points higher on their SAT tests (Shoda, Mischel & Peake 1990). That's tremendously higher. Furthermore, they had higher competence and less moodiness than the four-year-olds who ate the marshmallows immediately.

If you can learn how to choose to take control of your own feelings, if you can empower your brain to make choices that are best for your long-term benefit, the payoff is going to be great. And I'm not just talking about the payoff of choosing love and finding yourself someday in the glory of God's presence. Even without religious considerations, choosing love or other positive feelings, moment by moment, will eventually have a payoff—an increased competence and better treatment, or handling, of moodiness.

PART 3

ACHIEVING THE LOVE SKILLS

CHAPTER 8

THE PSYCHOLOGY OF LOVE

I've covered the barriers and the challenges to love. I've also covered the important role of constantly making decisions for acts of love. So now I'm going to explore past psychological concepts of love and explore what to add to the mix of these theories. It starts with the word *psyche*. Psyche is the term from ancient Greece upon which the word *psychology* is based—the study of the psyche. And Greek mythology has a story where Cupid loved a princess by the name of Psyche (Apuleius, second century AD). Furthermore, when we look at what they meant by the word—psyche meant the human soul, the spirit or mind, and *breath*. They believed that when a person breathed his or her last breath, that not only the spirit, but the soul and the mind, left the body as well. This ancient word seems very vague, however, and it is still vague today.

The word *love* is also vague today. Leo Buscaglia (1972) indicated that a lot of people had told him that love is nothing but prejudicial, superstitious, unscientific bosh. Only now is psychology using science to uncover the nature of love, with limited success. In the past, it's been the venue of poets. For example, the poet Rumi, in his book titled *The Book of Love: Poems of Ecstasy and Longing,* is quoted as saying, "Love is an open secret, the most obvious thing in the world, and the most hidden, with no why to how it keeps its mystery" (Barks 2003).

I indicated earlier that I hope I don't define "love." Part of the reason why love is so difficult to define is that asking different people what love is could get almost any kind of an answer. The reason is because of the nature of human beings themselves.

Remember Buckminster Fuller said that human beings are not nouns. They're verbs (Seiden 2013). I agree with him. I believe that people are ever-changing verbs, trying to be nouns, trying to turn other people into nouns. Furthermore, people constantly attempt to morph the words *to love* into a noun, as if someone could hold it within one's grasp. Love isn't such an easy concept. It's not such an easy act. And it is ever-changing, because people with their psyches are ever-changing.

Perhaps the reason many want to view themselves and love as nouns is because society treats people as human resources— as if all were objects to be used for the pleasure and profit of others. Buscaglia (1972) goes on to say that if a person wishes to love, the person must live love in action. When someone looks for love actions religiously, there are the eight Beatitudes in the Bible (Matthew 5:1–13) that would be a good guideline for how to behave, or act, in terms of love. One of those Beatitudes says, "Blessed are the clean of heart, for they will see God." There's that word again, *heart*. Clean of heart. It goes beyond chastity. We're talking about a heart that's eyeing itself toward God Himself. It's almost as if Jesus is saying, "Those that see God on this earth will be with him in the next earth."

Buscaglia also says that the loving person, "sees the continual wonder and joy of being alive ... there has never been the same sunset twice." We need to see each day as a new learning and add wonder and joy to that new learning. And to do so with a purity of heart.

"Love is a discipline" according to Eric Fromm (1956). According to Buscaglia, "Love is never complete in any person.

There's always room for growth." So it's a discipline, a growth. It's ever-changing. It involves wonder and joy. Albert Einstein indicates, "There are only two ways to live your life. One is as though nothing is a miracle. The other is as though everything is a miracle" (Einstein Goodreads.com). The wonder and joy of living—that's not a bad definition of love. It goes far beyond that. But perhaps it's that wonder and joy of being aware of God that's at the heart—the very soul—of love itself. Perhaps this was the light that I thought I saw in the eyes of those special people who loved me in my childhood.

Victor Frankl (1965) says that we have three layers of loving. The first one is the physical-attraction layer. Certainly, when we see somebody we're physically attracted to, all kinds of body hormones erupt. The person becomes the object of our focus. It's as if we just want to gaze into the person's eyes all the time. There's definitely a physical component to love.

However, if I'm attracted to a certain color hair, a certain figure, a certain physique—these are not unique to the person. I can find somebody else with that same color hair and the same body type that I'm attracted to. That doesn't make love very precious and rare. That's just the first layer of love.

Frankl goes on to say that second is the personality. Another one of the meanings of the word *psyche* is the personality structure of a person. And so, let's say that I like somebody who is an introvert, is demure, and appreciates beauty. In other words, I have a whole list of psychological traits and qualities that I'm attracted to. Just like the physical aspect of love, personalities are similar also. I can find somebody else who is an introvert, somebody else who appreciates beauty. There is nothing special or unique about this layer of love either.

Granted, it's fairly hard to find somebody who stimulates the physical attraction and the personality attraction at the same time. But it's possible. A person can find several people that meet those criteria. It's amazing how often people that get divorced and remarry find someone very similar to whom they were married in the first place, in terms of physical attributes and personality. So, if love is rare, Victor Frankl says we have to get to a third level, a spiritual level. We need to "love who the person is, as unique, irreplaceable and incomparable." We need to get to the ancient "psyche" of the person.

When Frankl was in the concentration camp at Dachau, he was subjected to dehumanizing conditions. Everything about those concentration camps reduced people to objects. Their names were immaterial. The only thing the Nazis did was use them for forced labor to the point of exhaustion and even death, with minor resources of food for survival. It was hard to continue on under those circumstances. And one day Frankl was having a particularly difficult time keeping himself going, spiritually. And then the idea of his wife came into his head. And he is quoted in his book *Man's Search for Meaning* (Frankl 1959): "I understand how a man who has nothing left in the world still knows bliss—be it only for a brief moment—in the contemplation of his beloved." Not in the contemplation of the physical attraction or the personality attraction, but the attraction to the spirit—the psyche—of his wife. When he chose, when he used that ability to choose where to focus, and focused on the love of his life, his wife—in those extreme circumstances—he experienced bliss. Christ has made such bliss available to our hearts.

It's been said that love is powerful. I think Victor Frankl shows in his experience that the power of love is present even in the harshest of human conditions. How can we tap into a spirit of love with our hearts that's that strong? We have trouble when somebody cuts us off on the freeway. How can we bring the power of love from our hearts into our daily living; to see rainbows, instead of concrete?

Once again, Eric Fromm (1956) states, "The practice of an art requires discipline." Still, when we look at love, and we look at the Christian life, the word that comes to my mind is *impossibility*. I don't see how Victor Frankl did it. He was tapping into something spiritual, something from God, in order to continue on under those circumstances. Something that's impossible without the spiritual life. God gives us the choice to love or not to love. I think it's the choice to enter into God, the basis of all miracles, the basis of all that's both natural and supernatural, the light shining in the darkness. First John 4:7–8 states, "Love is of God; everyone who loves is begotten by God and knows God. Whoever is without love does not know God, for God is love."

God is love. Synonyms. Wherever you use the word *love*, you can use the word *God*. Wherever you use the word *God*, you can use *love*. The title of this book could very well be, *Breathe Only God*.

So, when I'm saying to my wife, "I love you," I'm also saying that I take the love of God in me, and that love emanates to you. Wherever God is, there also is love.

And to go on with the scripture, God loved us and sent his son to expiate our sins. And I don't like to think of sin in terms of guilt and badness. I like to think of it in terms of weakness, of a lack of love.

He sent His Son to bring us love, so that we can enter into love. And the scripture says, "God is love, and whoever remains in love remains in God and God in him" (1 John 4:16). That scripture is the closest I can get to a definition of love. How do you define the infinite? Love, if love is God, is infinite. It has an infinite power, and when we ignore love, we feel a tremendous vacuum.

I was once told that the opposite of love is not hatred, because with hatred we still have a connection with somebody. There's still an object that we are directing our feelings toward. The opposite of love is indifference, of not even caring, of acting as if the object doesn't even exist. I've been treated that way by people at times, and I'm sure I've treated some people that way at times. That is the moment when it is time for me to tap into my ability to choose, and to choose love, to choose to do what God commands.

People seek satisfaction in so many ways. When we're hungry, we eat food. The food tastes so good, feels so good to us, that we want more and more. If we have too much food, it doesn't feel so good. We feel stuffed; we feel lethargic. We might have indigestion. So, food has limits upon its satisfaction. Some of us drink alcohol for satisfaction. We get satisfaction from water. All of these provide only a temporary satisfaction. Matter of fact, the National Opinion Center survey research data shows that the United States has accumulated tremendous wealth—three times the per capita wealth in the last fifty years (Myers 2014). That's truly phenomenal. And yet, in those same fifty years, when we measure the satisfaction that people in America have had, there hasn't been an increase at all. We get satisfaction from love—not from wealth, not from things. We get love from Jesus Christ, our God, our Love. The answer isn't who will love me. The answer isn't, "How am I going to get love?" The answer is inside of us. How do I go about giving love? It is not in getting the universe to do what we want it to do. It's contributing to the universe what we can contribute that's unique only to ourselves.

Victor Frankl (1959) speaks to that. He says that we all have a unique feature—even people at a checkout stand. Let's say that there are three checkout stands in a grocery store. Those three checkers aren't checking groceries out exactly the same way. Some are faster than others. Usually, the interaction of the employee with the customer is very different between three different checkout personnel. We have a unique way of going about our living. This uniqueness comes from our meaning in life. We can choose a meaning in life, and whatever meaning in life we choose, the way it's defined is unique to us.

For example, I had a plumber once ask me, "Why do you teach psychology?"

And I said, "To love people. Why do you do plumbing?"

He said, "Same thing. To love people."

Then he went on to explain to me how fixing plumbing is

helping other people. As I indicated, it is not getting from the universe what we want. It's giving to the universe what it needs. Loving means to give love. Happiness is a byproduct of walking on that journey of love. That plumber did more than just plumb. He also connected with people. His behavior even reflects Erich Fromm's theory.

Erich Fromm (1956) talks about four fundamental elements of love. The first element is care. He defines that as "the act of concern for the life and growth of that which we love." This reflects back to what Frankl calls "spiritual love." What is the nature of the person or object that I choose to love? And how can I help to grow that?

Years ago I was exposed to the concept that if you want a new tree to grow, when it's planted in the ground, you don't reach down and grab that tree by the trunk and lift it up, saying, "Grow." If you do, you'll pull it out by its roots, and it will die. If you want that tree to grow, you provide just enough water. In the first place, you plant it where the sun exposure will be just right, and you make sure that the nutrients are available to it. It's the same thing about caring for those that we love. What does the person need to thrive in pursuit of the person's meaning in life? What does the person need, and how can you provide it, which is Fromm's second fundamental element of love: responsibility? By this he's not talking about assigning blame if someone doesn't do something. He's talking about the ability to respond to the needs, whether the other person expresses that need or doesn't express that need. That human being needs our response. All human beings need a response from someone. When that car cuts you off on the freeway, the driver is not even acknowledging your existence. The person is all caught up in himself and where he wants to go, and you're irrelevant. And perhaps that's why it angers so many of us so much.

Fromm's third fundamental element of love is respect. Respect basically means to let the other person grow in her own way and in her own manner. Prescribing how someone else's behavior should be is just respecting one's own opinion, not the other person's. Can an individual give others the freedom to think and to behave in their own ways? Can that individual grant them the dignity that's inherent in all human beings?

Someone is not really loved unless known and understood by someone else. Knowledge is the fourth fundamental element—a real understanding. To do this, we need to get outside of ourselves and into the very nature of the person that we love. We need to be less focused on ourselves and more focused on the other. Can you imagine loving that person who cut us off on the freeway? That's what we're called to do. I mean, what are we going to do? Speed up and pull him over and say, "Buddy, I just want you to know, I love you"? Well, sometimes something as simple as a smile shows it all. However, if love is from God, and if there's a spiritual component, love can emanate from our hearts to the hearts of the other people—even the ones who are treating us like objects, without respect, as if we don't even exist. St. Francis of Assisi once said, "Preach and preach often; and if you need to, use words" (Calvo 2015). Pope Francis is calling upon his church members to show more joy in their lives. Perhaps our nonverbal communication is the essential component—the central love-skill—that we need to practice. Nonverbally, we can make ourselves into a wonderful beacon for others to see that love is possible and still exists in this world that, otherwise, would be totally dark.

Another theorist is Sternberg (1986), and he came up with a triangle of love. He says that there are three components to love, and the first one is "liking" or "intimacy." We need to get close to the people we love. We need to develop a specialness to the relationship. When was the last time we did something special for somebody we love? Do we do enough special things for our children? Do we take the time to give of ourselves? Do we develop trust, so that we can be depended upon? All these are the elements of intimacy.

Second, Sternberg speaks of passion. There's an energy in a relationship of love. It can be physical attraction. It can be personality attraction, even spiritual attraction.

Finally, his third component of the triangle is commitment. Here I'm talking about all the things that go into investing into the relationship I have with the other person. When I'm committed, and a decision needs to be made, I go to the person I'm deciding with, and I decide together with him or her. Commitment: a long-lasting giving of oneself to another in relationship.

Now Sternberg goes further than this. He says you can mix any or all of these three elements. Let's say that you have the passion and the intimacy, for example. Mixing these two meets his definition for "romantic love." Passion is fleeting, but the other two are components that grow over time. Thus, since passion decreases over time, the romantic love is only for a relatively short period of time.

My final theorist is Helen Fisher, who is a biological anthropologist who bases her theory of love on scientific research (Brown, L., et al. 2013). She has identified four temperaments for love. These temperaments include being curious, cautious, logical, and empathetic. The point that I want to make from her theory, however, is that brain scans reveal four distinctly different areas of the brain that are activated when one warmly gazes upon the image of a loved one. These areas of the brain are associated with the chemicals of dopamine/epinephrine, serotonin, testosterone, and estrogen/oxytocin.

Fisher appears to have isolated a deeper understanding of how so many people interpret love to mean so many different things. She also sheds light on why there are so many theorists on the topic of love. My approach presented in this book is probably coming from the empathy/oxytocin part of my brain. So, if my ideas don't resonate with your heart, it doesn't necessarily mean that one of us is right. It probably means that we exercise different kinds of love.

So there are a lot of different ways of thinking about love. Frankl has layers, Buscaglia describes it as creativity, Fromm lists fundamental elements, Sternberg has components, and Fisher has four temperaments from four brain regions. But as I look at all of these, I see so many words. If love is a skill—and Fromm says just that—then what exercises are there to perform? With the skill of baseball, someone hits a lot of baseballs and catches a lot of baseballs. When someone practices the skill of love, just what are the skills to practice?

What calisthenics of love are there to be enjoyed? These words from theorists about mental constructs for love can all be guides for the various actions to practice in the name of love. We can develop skills of curiosity, caution, analysis, and empathy to employ in the loving of others. But how do we keep our minds clear—whichever of the various parts we use—when we're being challenged with the demands of the society in which we live? Could there be a universal skill that covers whatever type of love a person employs? The heart has the power to free various regions of the brain to do this. When we learn and practice this certain heart skill, we'll be practicing love itself.

CHAPTER 9

THE HEART IS THE BRIDGE

Leo Buscaglia (1972) quotes Thornton Wilder in his book *The Bridge of San Luis Rey*, "There is a land of the living and a land of the dead. The bridge is love: the only truth: the only survival."

Let's look a little bit at that land of the dead. This society is based on individualism, and we've seen it grow, while at the same time seeing religion in the family declining. This gives our young people a sense that they, as individuals, are the ones who are responsible for their failures. If they get jilted, for example, then they're the ones responsible for being rejected. In cultures that are more based on community, this self-blame, this diagnosis of major depression, is far less common (Tremmel 2009). That importance of having a relationship and cooperation is valued and infused into non-Western cultures.

Now, as a partial result of this individualism, an individual goes through life with failures and rejections that trigger the "fight or flight response," mentioned earlier (Cannon 1963). This response involves one segment of the nervous system, called the sympathetic nervous system. The sympathetic nervous system arouses the whole body, but mainly it arouses the heart. Blood pressure goes up and the heartbeat quickens, along with other bodily changes. Another separate part of the nervous system is called the parasympathetic nervous system. It's not just a letting go of the sympathetic accelerator; it's actually operating like a brake that is relaxing the heart and other systems (Childre & Martin 1999).

So, each one of us has this neurological system to relax our hearts. These two systems are designed to have a homeostasis. There needs to be a balance between the two. In our society of individualism, of performance and accomplishment, we're activating the sympathetic nervous system far more than the parasympathetic nervous system. This plays a big role—a giant role—in our rages and in our fears.

Each of us also has a part of our brains called the amygdala, which houses emotions and memories of emotions. When fear is triggered, a need to flee emerges—the flight part of fight or flight. When anger is triggered, a need to fight emerges.

It's even been said that loneliness—this lack of connection with other people that leaves oneself alone with the fight or flight response—is the root cause of neuroses and many psychoses (McWhirter 1990). We see this entire dynamic of being alone, fight and flight, in Neil Diamond's song, "*I am, I said.*" And I'd like to quote him here, "And I am lost, and I can't even say why, leaving me lonely still." People are going through life emotionally begging people to recognize who they are, in order to get that respect that Eric Fromm speaks about, respect that isn't even there.

Psychologist Brené Brown (2013), in her recording, *The Power of Vulnerability*, interviewed people about love. When she brought up the topic of love, the communication of the people she interviewed was about heartbreak and about how this heartbreak brings guilt and shame and fear—fight or flight response, sympathetic nervous system; the heartbeat, beating irregularly at a high rate. This lack of a belief in oneself or that one's self deserves love continues, keeping us disconnected from other people. The people who believed in themselves, and believed that they deserved love, were described as having courage. The root of the word *courage* means whole heart. Instead of saying,

"I am," like Neil Diamond's song, we need to be going through life saying, "You are," to people starving to be recognized and respected—forming a bond. I once heard a sermon about both heaven and hell metaphorically having large banquet tables with all the food that anyone would love to eat. Both tables, however, had utensils that were four feet long. In hell, bedlam broke out, with everyone trying to steal food off of other people's plates. In heaven, meanwhile, there was no bedlam. There was only peace as everyone was feeding someone else off of their plates. Love is a gift from someone, not something that we take away from someone.

Research shows us that when we massage and touch premature babies, they develop their brains more quickly, they gain weight more quickly, they leave the ICU more quickly, and they develop their senses and their speech patterns far better than those premature babies that are not handled (Field 2006). And we see similar results when we look at children growing up in institutions. Without that sense of belonging, they're extremely withdrawn. They're frightened—fight or flight response, sympathetic nervous system.

And those monkeys from the Harlows (Harlow, Harlow & Suomi 1971). The infant monkeys not only preferred cloth; they preferred being rocked. They preferred warmth when they were being fed. They found this more appealing.

Much of human communication involves touch and cuddling. When we touch, when we cuddle, when we connect physically as well as psychologically and emotionally, it forms within our hearts a secure base. Erik Erikson (1963) called it "basic trust." When infants see the world as predictable and trustworthy, they form a basic trust. Monkeys deprived of this sense of basic trust appear terrified.

The interesting thing is that studies of attachment have found that this basic trust predicts romantic styles later in life (Feeney 1990). So, let's say that an infant cries with a need. And let's say that the infant's need gets responded to. The message that the infant receives from the response is, "You exist. What do you need? I'll help supply it." A secure base, a basic trust, is formed between the caregiver and the child, if this is the predominant way of responding to that infant. This basic trust seems to be part of the infant's life all the way until he matures enough to enter into romantic relationships—when that basic trust reflects itself in the mature relationship. This is how pervasively love operates within the human species.

Hadden, et al. (2014) found that if the basic trust of the attachment was insecure, that the romantic attachment, years later, was also insecure. This is such an important part of who we are—this hunger to connect, to give love, rather than to receive love. Erich Fromm (1956) says that people strive to be loveable, as if it were possible.

The full answer lies in the achievement of interpersonal union, a fusion with another person in love. It is in loving that we become loveable. How backward that seems. Instead of saying, "I am," and demanding and telling people, "I am somebody," if, in turn, we say to others, "You are somebody," and communicate that we really recognize them by seeing their qualities, their "uniqueness," as Frankl says, then what happens? They acknowledge us. And we don't have to make the demand to be recognized.

Let's look at the land of the living from the Wilder reference. When looking at love, research shows warm and tingly feelings grow inside of their chests when people experience compassion (Haidt 2000). Compassion is physically sensed inside the chest, in the region of the body where the heart resides. The interesting thing is that when feeling connected, a person starts secreting a hormone called "oxytocin." Oxytocin was first discovered as a secretion of the mother during childbirth. The idea was that this hormone secretion prepared the mother and child for bonding with each other. So right there, during the birth process, hormones of bonding are being secreted. Since then it has been found that whenever feeling very close to somebody, we secrete oxytocin.

It's been found in men as well as women, and it's not only being secreted from the brain. Recent findings show that oxytocin is even secreted by the heart (Gimpl & Fahrenholz 2001).

The introduction to Leo Buscaglia's book *Love* indicates that even though we cannot define this infinite reality, he likes the quote of one of his students from his Love class. She said, "I find love much like a mirror. When I love another, he becomes my mirror, and I become his. And reflecting in each other's love we see infinity." What a beautiful quote. Infinity, love, God. These cannot be separated. They're all one and the same.

Psychology shows that simply perceiving other people creates fondness toward those people (Titchener 1910). All we need to do is to be exposed to somebody. And the tendency is for us to like them and to connect.

Love activates a reward system within the brain. Not only are oxytocin hormones secreted, but also neurotransmitters, chemicals within the brain, are secreted. Research shows that when pain is induced in subjects through the use of heat, the deeply-in-love university students feel significantly less pain when looking at pictures of their beloved (Younger, Park, Chatterjee & Mackey 2010). When connected, pain is dealt with far better than when alone.

Much like atoms are the basic units for matter, neurons are the basic units for nervous systems and for brains. Brains are mainly nerves composed of neurons. Humans are also wired to feel other people's pain through what's called mirror neurons. Mirror neurons were first discovered accidentally in psychology (Blakesee 2006). A monkey's brain was wired into biofeedback, and the experimenters went out to lunch. And when they came back, one of the assistants was still eating. Somebody noticed that the monkey's brain changed as the experimenter ate. In other words, when the experimenter experienced the taste, the pleasure of the food, the monkey had a mirror experience of the research assistant's brain for tasting the pleasure of that food. When people see another person experience extreme, sudden pain, they react partially as if it were them experiencing that pain.

Humans are connected through these mirror neurons. They're also connected through hormones. You and I are connected by the chemical messengers in our brains and the chemical messengers in our blood. In other words, God created us for connection. God created us for loving. When this connection is broken by us being ignored or ostracized, there is intense psychological pain (Williams 2001). This psychological pain is carried into society, onto freeways, into communication patterns with each other, and inside the individualistic culture, which then treats people as if they are exclusively human resources for use.

Instead, when we communicate, we need to communicate with love. We need to avoid falling into this routine of living and enter into the miracle that Einstein describes. There are miracles all around us. Every human being is a unique miracle to be experienced. We need to get out of the routine and start interacting with these miraculous people.

I like to think of an interaction itself as another person, in a way. There's the other person and there is me. This imaginary third person, which I call the "inter-person." Are we loving the inter-person? Are we loving, caring for, respecting, and knowing our inter-persons and what inter-persons need for our relationships to continue? We have an inter-person, not only with the important people in our lives, but also with God.

Instead of asking the same question each day like, "Hi. How has your day gone? What did you experience?" People need to start asking creative questions like, "Was there a time today when you experienced love? What did you notice in God's creation, in nature, today, that gave you a warm, glowing feeling inside? What more *could* you have done to get that feeling? When you were in school today, child of mine, did you raise your hand? If you were to raise your hand, what would you have asked? If you don't know what to ask, let's get together, sit down, and figure out what kind of a question you could ask in class."

Love is so creative. It's exciting. It's connecting. It's what we're wired to be. It's who we are. We are a bonding, attaching species. God created us that way, so we can bond and attach with Him. The greatest of all commandments: "You shall love the Lord, your God, with all your heart, with all your being, with all your strength, and with all your mind, and your neighbor as yourself" (Luke 10:27). We are to bond with love itself. We are to bond with all that we are. We are to bond with our neighbors. And it is the foremost commandment, on which all other commandments are based.

This creativity that love requires for our communication, for our actions of love, for our thoughts, and for our feelings, truly reflects Erich Fromm's belief that love is an art. My position, being that God is love, requires us to give love to God and others, as the commandments state, in order to receive love from God and others. The key to this giving creatively lies literally, not metaphorically, in our hearts. According to current neuroscientists, the heart is far more than just a pump for our blood (Elliott 2006).

One Internet site, the Christian Bible Reference Site, shows that the word *heart* appears approximately 726 times in the New American Standard Bible. This would lead me to interpret that the heart is one of the primary centers of Christianity. Consider just a few of those 726 biblical references.

In Proverbs 28:14, "Those who harden their hearts fall into evil."

John 14:1, "Do not let your hearts be troubled. You have faith in God; have faith also in me." It's Jesus comforting his disciples.

In Luke 24:38, "Why are you troubled? And why do questions arise in your hearts?'"

And finally, Mark 2:8, "Why are you thinking such things in your hearts?"

Now, if we are to take these verses literally, the human heart is capable of becoming callous, chaotic, and indifferent. The heart directly affects our senses and our understandings. We can doubt God in our hearts. In short, we can think with our hearts, as well as with our brains.

A 1984 book titled *Neurocardiology* by Armor and Ardell, relates that neuroscientists have found clusters of forty thousand and more neurons within the human heart. And Armor and Ardell refer to this as the "brain in the heart."

It's long been a mystery how the human fetus in the womb can begin its heartbeat way before the brain even forms. The "brain in the heart" explains this phenomenon. The brain isn't telling the heart to beat. The heart is telling the heart to beat. Furthermore, this tiny "brain in the heart" communicates independently of the cranial brain in a manner that impacts our cortex. Our cortex is where our brains think, analyze, make decisions, and form judgments. In short, modern science has found that the heart can strongly influence the thought processes of our cranial brains.

In 1670, Pascal wrote, "The heart has its reasons, which reason does not know" (Pascal 1670). I'm talking here about scientists discovering that the Bible, religions, and the poets have been correct all along—that love indeed comes from the heart.

Let's look at Proverbs 3:3–6: "Do not let love and fidelity forsake you; bind them around your neck; write them on the tablet of your heart. Then will you win favor and esteem before God and human beings. Trust in the Lord with all your heart, on your own intelligence do not rely; In all your ways be mindful of him, and he will make straight your paths." I read this to mean that God is spotlighting in the scriptures that love coming forth from our hearts is to rule our cranial brains.

Could that be what's wrong with modern society today? Science came along, and people started looking at parts of the whole. Instead of perceiving entire wholes, they broke everything down into one question each and crept our knowledge forward by separating everything. People started believing that the mind and the body were two different things—and they are not.

The heart has the capacity to rule the brain. They are connected—not separate. Does the heart really have the power to rule the brain? If so, we then need to tap into love in our hearts and send that love from our hearts to God so that the light of love emanating from God can show us a path to Him. Elliott (2006) describes that humans have this skill potential.

Elliott states that we increase sympathetic arousal when we increase our breathing frequency. We increase our parasympathetic system when we decrease breathing frequency and depth. A third bodily system is also intertwined. Our heart rates also increase and decrease in synchrony. So, breathing, nervous system and our heart rates are all intimately intertwined. Breathing, however, yields much more easily to conscious control.

To quote from Matthew 14:29, when Jesus was walking on water to the boat, Peter asked if he could come to him. Jesus said, "Come." Peter got out of the boat and began to walk on the water toward Jesus. But when he saw how [strong] the wind was he became frightened; and, beginning to sink, he cried out, 'Lord, save me!' Immediately Jesus stretched out his hand and caught him, and said to him, 'O you of little faith, why did you doubt?'" Why did Peter look at the danger instead of at the path to Jesus? I believe that the thoughts in his mind were taking hold of the faith in his heart.

One of the times I got lost in meditation, I was really worrying about a major decision I had to make, that would impact my entire life. I was sitting on this cliff overlooking the ocean, and the sun was setting. Like the sun does on a clear day, the sun reflected off of the ocean water. There was this glittering, golden path shining from the shore all the way to the sun. In my mind's eye I thought if instead of the star sun, that were the Son of God, it would be the Son of God showing me the path, the "bridge," of getting to Him. And I was thinking, you know, there are a lot of times when I take my eyes off of Christ, and I find myself basically sinking. So if I was to look at something else and start walking in that direction—assuming I could walk on water like Peter did—I would sink. I would be off of the light-reflection path to the sun (Son). But all I would have to do is look back at the sun and that glittering, golden path would still be there. I would still have a bridge to divine guidance.

So I've shown from other scriptures that we can doubt with our heart. We know that we can fall away from love. We know that we're finite and at times incapable of love. Just how important is the heart in love? Well, there's a study at the University of California, Davis. The study appears in *Science Daily* (2012), a journal article written by Emilio Ferrer, as well. He studies couples who are in romantic relationships, and what he found in this study, by monitoring the heart rates and the breathing, or respiration, he found that couples in love would get their heart rates in sync with each other, and that they would breathe in and out at the same intervals. When two individuals were not a couple, their hearts didn't show the synchrony, nor did their breathing match. When we love, the beating of our hearts unites. I have seen other stories that show synchrony between humans and dogs, and between humans and horses.

What about when we leave our hearts, when we leave this love, when we break the connection with the people that we love, when we break the synchronicity between God and others? I once heard somebody play with the word *meanness*. And the way they played with it, they said that cruelty comes from indifference. It comes from "me-ness." In other words, sometimes we can get so locked up inside of ourselves and the needs that we have, that we lose sight of our God, and we lose sight of our neighbor.

It's described in Psalm 109:22: "For I am poor and needy; my heart is pierced within me."

And Proverbs warns in 4:23 to "With all vigilance guard your heart, for in it are the sources of life."

And 2 Thessalonians 3:5, "May the Lord direct your hearts to the love of God and to the endurance of Christ."

When we leave love, our hearts actually show different heartbeat patterns from working in accord to working in discord with the other body systems. Could it be that the peoples in ancient times were more tuned into these physiological messages from the heart? We know that Aristotle believed that the mind or psyche, which included the spirit, resided in the heart. And evidently, this belief was fairly prevalent in almost all ancient civilizations (Childre 1999).

In Ezekiel 36:26 God says, "I will give you a new heart, and a new spirit I will put within you. I will remove the heart of stone from your flesh and give you a heart of flesh." I believe that this "heart of flesh instead" is a more caring and loving heart. Do we have a natural, loving heartbeat and a less natural, less loving heartbeat as well? Perhaps science is showing us that that's exactly what's happening: a heartbeat that is in cooperation with the body and a heartbeat that is not. And how does the less natural heartbeat look in our lives?

CHAPTER 10

THE NEED TO REWIRE
OUR BRAINS

We have studies on learned helplessness, where we put dogs or fish in a situation where they cannot have control to meet their needs—for example, a need for eating (Seligman 1975). What was found was that, when they're deprived of being able to help themselves, they learn helplessness. They can actually starve to death with plenty of food around. How "unnatural" is that? We can train animals to believe that eating food will harm them, and they'll actually die of starvation. This demonstrates how our sense of control is so important.

Think of how this may apply to the control of our emotions. Think of the possibility of being able to control our thoughts and feelings through our breathing and therefore, through our hearts. Situations wouldn't have control of our feelings. Rodin (1982) even found that nursing home patients died sooner when they had less control of their daily lives than another group of nursing patients who had more control of their lives.

Then there's a study of 180 Catholic nuns (Danner, Snowden & Frissen 2001). The researchers had the nuns write brief autobiographies when they were twenty-two years old, and again in old age. Since they were all nuns in the service of the church, they all had very similar lives. The autobiographies, written at age twenty-two, that happened to show expressions of happiness, love, and other positive feelings predicted that these nuns would die, on an average, seven years later than those not expressing positive feelings. And at age eighty, 24 percent of them had died, as opposed to 54 percent of those that were expressing negative emotions. The theory is that happiness, love, and positive feelings neutralize the stress response in bodies that over time can wear the bodies down and shorten lives.

Psychology is now beginning to look into positive feelings. A whole discipline is emerging called positive psychology, and a small part of this new discipline is linked to the "coherent" heartbeat pattern. William James, the American psychologist of the nineteenth century, taught that if an individual wants to have a certain feeling, he should do it first in his body (James 1890). For example, if you want to be happy, try smiling. You might try it right now. Put a great big grin on your face and see if it doesn't improve your mood. That was some of the earliest psychology about positive feeling. Depression, and the negative thinking that goes together with depression, reside in the right side of brains; whereas, positive emotions and positive thinking reside mainly in the left side of brains (Harmon-Jones, Abramson, Sigelman, Bohlig, Hogan & Hogan-Jones, C. 2002). One theory holds that if someone practices using just that one part of the brain, and does not practice using the other part, a kind of a use-it-or-lose-it phenomenon takes place. The parts of our brains that we use grow, and the parts of our brains that we do not use atrophy or shrink in size.

So, here we are in this society where we can't go five minutes without a stressor hitting us, and we're using over and over again, moment by moment, this right frontal-lobe negative-thinking, negative-feeling part of our brains. And that's the part of our brains that we are expanding.

Researchers also know that emotional responses follow two

pathways throughout the brain (LeDoux 2002). All perceptions, except the perception of smell, go to a part of the brain called the thalamus, which is like a switchboard. So whatever is experienced goes to this thalamus switchboard in the brain that sends it to the head, the cortex, where a person thinks about what she is perceiving.

So, if you could imagine yourself driving down the road, and all of a sudden the light changes to amber, this perception goes to the switchboard. The switchboard says, "Think about it, cortex." And in your brain you think, *Is this dangerous? Should I hit the brake, or should I step on the gas?* Whatever you choose, you're going to have an emotional response, "Step on it!" You're going to increase your arousal to get through that intersection. Or, "Hit the brakes!" or even "Hit the brakes fast!" Ditto.

What's happening is that the cortex is also sending the message to a part of your brain called the amygdala. The amygdala is where feeling memories reside in the brain. Now, neurologists have also found that sometimes when something is perceived, it bypasses the cortex and goes straight to that amygdala. The amygdala says to the body, "Go into the sympathetic nervous system and trigger that fight or flight response without it being conscious" (Van der Kolk 2013).

If you could imagine a spider dropping down on your arm—if you're like me, you're going to jump without thinking about it. That's the second pathway. Well, a lot of this direct-to-the-amygdala experience has to do with these negative experiences we've had over and over and over and over again. After a while, we don't have to think about it. After a while, if someone cuts you off on the freeway, you hit the brakes without *consciously* thinking to yourself, "Should I hit the brakes this time?"

If you're going to rewire your brain so that you can live longer, like those happy Catholic nuns, you need to interrupt that process that's going on in the amygdala (Salovey 1990). Unfortunately, I do not believe that the power of positive thinking can do that.

This is because the amygdala—that emotion center of the brain—sends far, far more messages to the cortex—the thinking part of our brain—than it receives (Van der Kolk 2013). So the feelings control thinking more so than the other way around. It's easier for your thoughts to be hijacked by your feelings. And it's not easy for thoughts to control feelings. What seems faster to you—your feelings or your thoughts?

Humans can appraise events as either harmless or dangerous so quickly that they're not even consciously aware of it, when the amygdala gets involved. Our amygdalae must be giant in our society that we live in today, because of the phenomenon that some call, "Use it or lose it." Psychology also has one of the oldest findings called the "feel-good-do-good" phenomenon (Harbaugh, Mayr & Burghart 2007). Experimental subjects were prompted into feeling happy. The likelihood of them doing a goodness for other people increased dramatically with the happy feelings. Feeling happy is, therefore, a pathway to actions of love.

I remember years ago reading a study where a coin was put on the sidewalk. If a student found it and proceeded down the sidewalk, or didn't find it and proceeded down the sidewalk, the other part of the experiment would have somebody else drop their papers all over the sidewalk. Well, more people who had found the coin helped that other person to pick up those papers than did the ones who did not even notice the coin. Why: the feel-good-do-good phenomenon. What needs to be done is to make people happy by doing good.

We need to practice our happy feelings. We need the amygdala to believe that things are happy. We also know that when we make charitable donations, the reward centers in our brains become activated (Seligman, Steen, Park & Peterson 2005). In other words, it feels good to love other people.

Positive psychology suggests that we keep daily gratitude journals. In religion we have often heard the statement, "Count your blessings." Can you count your blessings at the end of every day? Think of the impact—if you're going to sleep being happy—the impact that feeling will have on your sleep. I have actually learned how to cure decades of insomnia this way in my own life.

A speaker once came to my institution by the name of Chuck Wahl (2016). Chuck Wahl is legally blind, and he was an instructor at Bakersfield College in Bakersfield, California. He was in a car that was being driven to his class for him one day, and he was listening to the radio. On the radio came the message, "Well, it's happened again. We have news of a random act of violence."

And he said to himself, "Why can't we have news about random acts of kindness?" And so, he made the assignment in his class that day to go out and commit random acts of kindness upon other people—kind of a pass-it-forward idea, but before the *Pay It Forward* movie came out. Chuck wound up on national television, and he has appeared in national magazines. By following his idea, I have taken it upon myself to make that same assignment to my classes and for them to write their responses. Invariably, the students talk about how good it made them feel to do a random act of kindness for somebody else. And what is doing the opposite of this like?

I focused on the negative aspects of life over a large portion of my life after being terrified by a work situation. After that negative experience, which involved an abuse of authority, I went on a quest to fight the abuse of authority wherever I was involved with it. If I lost a fight for "the cause," at least I'd go down swinging. To make a long story short, I stressed myself so much over the years that I eventually found myself unconscious in the trauma unit of a hospital with what the doctors labeled "a heart event."

For three days in the intensive care unit, I meditated the stress away and then asked myself a crucial question: "John, where did you go wrong?" The fight was a good and worthy one for the principle of justice. Finally, I asked, "When was the last time I was really psychologically together, and what was I doing differently?" It all came down to my focus. I used to focus on building what

I love, and I had turned my gaze to the "great fight" for justice. Upon this realization, I formed a mantra of sorts for the rest of my life, and I have repeated it to myself countless times since: "Instead of fighting what I hate, build what I love!" Over the years, I've learned that this focus of building what I love has done more to fight injustice than all those years of lost energies that had led me to my "heart event."

My mantra appears to me to be at the heart of Martin Seligman's *Positive Psychology* (2005). A great fighter for justice put it this way, "I have decided to stick to love … Hate is too great a burden to bear" (King and Washington 1991).

I have also been taught a method for practicing positive feelings, and it involves changing my breathing and thus, my heartbeat. I was taught the method of how to change my heartbeat by reading a book called *Transforming Stress* by Childre and Rozman (2005). I read that book, and the first thing that I did was to throw it into the trash can. I thought, *This is baloney. The stuff in this book can't all happen. Nothing is that good for conquering stress.* I thought that I had tried everything—meditation, deep-muscle relaxation, yoga—and still, I had a heart attack. But then I went back and got that book, and I said to myself, "If this were true, I could actually change my blood pressure." And indeed, eventually I did change my blood pressure. By following what is in *Transforming Stress,* I lowered my blood pressure medications by 50 percent. I'm not saying here that the book works for everyone, but it sure worked for me.

But before I go further with that experience, I want to tell you a story about going to San Bernardino. After reading the book, I practiced the method that's in that book. I had practiced it for weeks, and I could not get the heartbeat pattern that was supposed to appear on their device. Later, I learned that I just wasn't breathing correctly. That really got to me because I've always been able to master biofeedback, whether it is affecting my perspiration on my fingers or my muscle tensions. But with this particular machine, I could not get my heartbeat pattern to follow. The end of the school year came—which, in itself, is a relief—and I found myself driving to San Bernardino. When I got outside of the town of Bishop, California—which is in a stark desert—the drive got kind of boring. I thought, *Hey, I'm going to practice that breathing method.* So, I started doing the method, and for some reason this time it worked. I was driving along, and all of the sudden a tremendous feeling of love and peace entered into my heart. And I went, "Whoa, this must be it! This has got to be it." But I didn't have my device with me, so I couldn't verify it. I have since found other similar devices that also help. I said to myself, "Well, whether it's it or not, it feels so good, I'm going to continue doing it." One of the biggest parts of that experience that led me to think, *Whoa*, was the realization that I could quit struggling so much in my life with the darkness of a world that I perceived as unloving. This love was like a brilliant explosion coming out of my own heart, due to the breathing. I was in control … finally! My heartbeat was under control by willing my breathing to be a certain way. A goal of finding peace for my life, which I had pursued for a lifetime, was finally achieved.

So, for about an hour and a half, I continued practicing this breathing/heart technique. I got to the motel, where I had reserved a room. That motel attempted to frustrate me more than any other motel that I've ever stayed at. What occurred to me there often makes people angry, even when I just tell them the story. They don't even have to experience it, and they get angry. I walked in, and they told me that they didn't have my reservation. I said, "Well, I paid for it."

And they said, "Well, show us your Internet printout."

I said, "I don't have one. Can I get on your machine, and I'll print it out?"

"No, you can't have access to our machine."

Well, long story short, it took me an hour and a half to find me a printer at a copy center in a different hotel. So I went back with my receipt, and I showed it to the clerk. And he said, "Huh!" and gave it back to me.

I said, "Well, do I get in?"

And he said, "No, you're still not in our records."

Why did they make me go look for that receipt? I thought.

What amazed me was that, throughout my entire life, I would uncontrollably hit the roof with anger in such a situation. Christ says in the Scripture, to "not let the sun set on your anger" (Ephesians 4:26). And I used to get angry at God, because, "How do I not let the sun set on my anger?" I didn't know how to do it. Psychology recommends relaxing and changing your thoughts, but those techniques never really worked for me. Once my anger was triggered, I experienced it as though the anger had a life all of its own.

But here I am, going through this nightmare to check into a hotel—all I wanted was a swim, and I couldn't get to that swimming pool for hours. Three hours after I arrived there, the receipt came in from the reservation company. They let me in, and I went up to bed and fell right to sleep.

Now, my entire life—you have to appreciate this—*my entire life* I would have spent hours cussing out that hotel in my head, staying awake trying to stop my mind from keeping me from going to sleep. Here I was even having the control to feel positive through the whole experience. I was feeling and projecting compassion toward the hotel clerk. I was finally following what the Bible teaches about anger.

How did I do that? It didn't come from great inspiration from a speaker. It didn't come from a life of holiness. It came from the simple breathing technique that Elliott (2006) says leads to the resonance of breathing with the nervous system and heart. This technique is what I believe to be an important skill of love. My practice of this skill has helped me immensely to love others better.

CHAPTER 11

THE POWER OF POSITIVE FEELING

This breathing/heart technique brings to my mind a song by Neil Diamond titled, "Be." There is one line in the song that says, "Sing as a song in search of a voice that is silent." I've had an ache in my heart—an ache for something that seemed nameless, an ache for something that seemed timeless and silent. And when I wanted to speak of it, I couldn't come up with a voice, because the ache was silent. As strange as this might sound, Neil Diamond's song spoke to that.

So, we find the idea of finding love inside of us to heal our hurts in art, like in song. François de La Rochefoucauld (1959), an author, puts it this way: "What the superior man seeks is in himself; what the small man seeks is in others." I seem to have been seeking a sense of being loved from others, when all along it was inside me—I just needed this technique to get to it.

We find this voice that I was seeking and which is almost silent in Kings, where Elijah was told to go to a mountain and wait for Yahweh (1 Kings 19:12–13). All kinds of things came to him when he was on the mountain—a hurricane, an earthquake, ravaging fire. The Scripture says that Yahweh was not in any of these. And the quote continues, "After the fire, a light silent sound. When he heard this, Elijah hid his face in his cloak and went out and stood at the entrance of the cave. A voice said to him ..."

We need to quiet our hearts in order to quiet our minds in this world of turmoil, efficiency, and speed—where everything is getting faster and faster. And we need to be able to take peace and a joy into that insane world, and somehow, hold on to it, for our own stress management, for our own spirituality, but mainly for us to be ready when the times come for us to love one another. People don't appear to be hearing His whisperings on freeways.

Yahweh wasn't in the storms or the fire. He was in that quiet voice. The peace is expressed in song, literature, and religion, and it's also found in psychology. I believe that Abraham Maslow once said that self-actualized people are calm, like a grandfather clock, ticking back and forth, one second at a time, while surrounded by a hurricane (Maslow 1968). That's what this breathing/heart technique has brought to my mind: That goal that I had for my life—to tick like that grandfather clock when everything around me was going insane—that's what I wanted. And to quote Neil Diamond again, "And we dance to a whispered voice, overheard by the soul, undertook by the heart," while the world around us appears insane by comparison.

Proverbs 12:25 states, "Worry weighs down the heart, but a kind word gives it joy."

Colossians 3:15 indicates, "And let the peace of Christ control your hearts, the peace into which you were also called in one body."

The secret to loving is in our hearts, in our physiological hearts, not just in our metaphorical hearts. And how do we get there? First, let's look at breathing in Scripture. I never knew this, but the term *Holy Spirit* comes from a word meaning "breath." To the ancient Greek—and I don't know, perhaps to the Hebrews— mind, soul, and breath all meant the same thing. Remember, the Greeks called it "psyche" (Apuleius, second century AD). When the last breath left the body, it represented the parting of the soul.

In Genesis 2:7, "then the Lord God formed the man out of the dust of the ground and blew into his nostrils the breath of life, and the man became a living being." When God was breathing into the nostrils of Adam, I don't think it's just life that he was breathing into Adam. He was breathing Himself into Adam. He was breathing love into Adam. So God first gave life and love to our species through breath. If we are to return that love back to God, or to pass it on to others, doesn't it make sense that we breathe love, when we look at it in this context? *Spirit* means breath. When we love one another, aren't we sharing God with one another? If God is truly love, then I think that's what it must be.

Just as our hearts can synchronize with the Lord, so may our breathing.

Colossians 3:12, 14–15 states, "Put on then, as God's chosen ones, holy and beloved, heartfelt compassion, kindness, humility, gentleness, and patience … And over all these put on love, that is, the bond of perfection. And let the peace of Christ control your hearts …"

Throughout the gospel, in several places, Jesus says, "Peace be with you." After his resurrection, when he went to the apostles, he sent them forth to preach. In John 20:22 it says, "And when he had said this, he breathed on them and said to them, 'Receive the holy Spirit.'"

Again, Proverbs 3:13 says, "Do not let love and fidelity forsake you; bind them around your neck; write them on the tablet of your heart."

With a heart that was stuck in fear and anger, at times I could enter into this feeling of love. But how do I bind it around my neck? How do I make it a part of my every moment in life—which would be the Christian's goal? How do I keep that anger and fear from resuming its life within my heart?

A simple breathing/heart technique, which was verified by scientific technology, changes the pattern of the beat of the heart and makes it resonate with the nervous system. This technique, when practiced, empowers an individual to make kindness and truth become a part of him. John 14:27 tells us, "Do not let your hearts be troubled or afraid."

Philippians 4:8, says "Finally, brothers, whatever is true, whatever is honorable, whatever is just, whatever is pure, whatever is lovely, whatever is gracious, if there is any excellence and if there is anything worthy of praise, think about these things." From this Philippians quote, I want to show you that he is talking about our minds, not about our hearts. I indicated earlier that the mind can have positive thoughts on the left side of the brain, or negative thoughts on the right side of the brain. As indicated in part 2, Barbara Frederickson (1998) studied the impact of happiness on people's lives. She indicates that humans spend much more time thinking on negative events than on positive events. We are in the grips of fear and anxiety in this society. Our minds need to be filled with those things that are pure. Our minds need to be filled with love.

Let's begin to look at just what this breathing technique entails. We need to choose to breathe at a rate that Elliott (2006) has scientifically found to be positively synchronous with the heart. The point at which most of my students fail to maximize the benefit has to do with making the breathing pattern habitual, so that it doesn't constantly require a choice. Behavioral psychologists teach us that we can strengthen behaviors, like breathing habits, with positive reinforcement. In other words, when behaviors are followed by something pleasant, then those behaviors occur more frequently. So, I propose that we recall positive, inspirational experiences while practicing the breathing pattern. This is a variation on other techniques used in other psychologies and disciplines.

I have fond memories of sitting on my grandmother's lap. When I was on her lap as a child, it was all love coming from her. Nobody would mess with me, because nobody would mess with Grandma. It's a place of safety. And to this day, I can still feel the love of my grandmother while she taught me what the ten commandments meant. When I was a teenager, my grandmother was gone. I had a pet golden retriever that I'd share my problems with. And just from the expressions on his face, I felt a bond with him, a bond of caring that was coming from the animal. When I turn my perceptions toward pets, like St. Francis of Assisi teaches, I have positive and happy feelings. Don't you? The perceptions don't even have to be real. It can be a spiritual movie or a book where my heart just leaps for joy when I read or see the happy rendering. There's a scene from *Ben Hur* that does this for me. And all that I have to do is remember that scene and I re-experience the presence of God. So, what I want you to do is to find the most powerful feeling memory of a spiritual experience that you have had that can trigger you into that state of peace and joy, whatever it is. For me, I'm going to pick that golden retriever. His memory puts a warm, glowing feeling upon me. The peace of God flowed through that dog to me.

The next thing has to do with changing brain-wave patterns. How many people wake up in the middle of the night and try to turn off their minds from going on and on and on? I did a baseline with myself, and my insomnia was one-third of all my nights—I'd wake up worrying for a half-hour or more. I wonder how many are doing that. How do we stop our minds? Perhaps our minds can't stop our minds, because we need something more powerful. Well, our brains have different brain-wave patterns when we're thinking words and considering actions. They call those waves a beta brain-wave activity. It's that conversation that's going on in our minds. We also have a brain-wave pattern called alpha waves. These waves, or ways of thinking, don't include words. If you've ever lain down on the ground and looked up at the clouds going by without a word in your head—just focusing on all sensation: smell, temperature—that was probably an alpha brain-wave pattern.

When I was a teenager playing pool, I found that if I was thinking beta brain waves, I couldn't make a very good pool shot. I had to think, *Now, where do I want to hit the cue ball with the cue? Where do I want the cue ball to connect with the target ball? Does that target ball need to bounce off the bumper to get to the hole? If so, just where would I want it to bounce?* I had all these thoughts. But after I had those thoughts, I would stop them and just rub the felt of the pool table. I'd get into a state where I would do what I call "touch thinking"—alpha brain waves—sensing the felt texture. And then I would feel the cue in my hands and fingers. And then I would think with movement, rather than words. When I did that, I could hit great pool shots all the time.

One of the things that we need to do is to get into this sensing-without-conversation part of our brains for the breathing practice. At first, I wasn't too successful at that. But as I've practiced and practiced, I've learned more and more how to shift. And as the power of my heart through breathing correctly gained in the ability to control my mind, I also got to the point where now I don't have insomnia anymore.

So, let's start by putting that spiritual experience feeling to the side for a while. Elliot's research indicates that our breathing needs to be "coherent." He defines this as "...breathing synchronously at the specific frequency of 1 cycle in approximately ~ 12b seconds with comfortable depth," and that "it results in autonomic nervous system balance, cardiopulmonary resonance, and coherence of the autonomic nervous system rhythm." To translate this into simpler language, it involves inhaling for five to six seconds and exhaling for five to six seconds. I went to my app store on my smartphone and searched for "breathing metronome." I found several apps that can help me to breathe rhythmically for a five-second inhale and a five-second exhale. Other devices that show heartbeat or breathing patterns are also described on the internet from the American Institute of Stress (www.stress.org). After I get the rhythm going, I just reinforce that breathing pattern with my past inspirational feelings and breathe while experiencing the peace and joy of the Lord. For me, I practiced Elliott's technique several times a day for five minutes each. After seven weeks, it was an automatic habit of peace and joy that my acquaintances all noticed in me. I know from counseling for changing many different habits over the years that we're all different in how long we have to practice a new pattern.

These are the calisthenics of love, the skills to be practiced until they become ever-present and automatic. They require the focus of alpha brainwave states for the breathing and inspirations. I practiced this every time I remembered to do so for each day until it became my new, normal way of breathing and feeling. It was then that I had a tool to go back to sleep every night when I would awaken. It was then that I could drive on a freeway in such a way that it became a welcome break from the activities of my days. Finally, I was shifting from the negative, right-brain-hemisphere to the positive, left-brain-hemisphere.

First John 4:18 says, "There is no fear in love, but perfect love drives out fear." I have used this technique with hundreds of students, and well over a hundred students have conquered the fear of mathematics in our therapeutic sessions and in my classrooms. From this technique I take them into our college laboratories. We monitor coherent breathing. Their heartbeats get projected onto the screen of the computer and in a matter of minutes—literally a few minutes—these students learn how to change their heartbeat patterns through synchronized breathing. The patterns change from a chaotic speeding up and slowing down to an organized speeding up and slowing down. It would be several accelerations, followed by several decelerations. In other words, we would momentarily take time for the sympathetic arousal to occur from the sympathetic nervous system, and then take a little more time for the parasympathetic nervous system relaxation to kick in. Every minute that we're in coherence, our sympathetic and parasympathetic nervous systems are working together, and this phenomenon of a coherent breathing/heartbeat pattern literally drives fear away. I've used this in treating phobias with remarkable results. I know a marriage and family therapist who's using it to bring love to couples in his couples' therapy practice, as well.

Meditate about this quote from Jeremiah 31:33: "I will place my law within them, and write it upon their hearts; I will be their God, and they shall be my people."

It took me two weeks, practicing the breathing three to four times a day for five minutes, before I could display my breath/heart synchronicity. Yet with my students, with their younger hearts, I see them change their heartbeat patterns in a total of five to ten minutes of practicing this technique. I continued practicing this technique for two months. It felt so good to me, so relieving—so what I was looking for—it was like that "song in search of a voice that was silent." After two and a half months of three to four times a day for five minutes or less, I experienced a brand new breathing habit that literally keeps my heart at peace on an ongoing basis. That shift changed what was normal for me from a feeling of fear and anxiety to a feeling of love in God's presence. Peace was truly with me. Kindness and truth were bound around my neck. I was breathing love as a habit.

There would be times during the day when I would leave it, but eventually I could use the breath/heart skill and get back to coherence in the matter of half-a-minute or so. Some life events would come that were so big, and I'd lose it for even a day or two. But I would always do the breathing exercises when I would think of them, even though I couldn't get the inspirational feeling to reinforce it. Maybe I couldn't reach what it felt like to be on my grandmother's lap because I was dealing with the big problem of the day. But after several days of persistence, I would come back to the peace and joy of the Lord. And each time I hit a situation that was too great for me, my persistence would whittle it down, and it would take a situation even stronger than the earlier one to rob me of my peaceful breathing.

Now, take this phenomenon and think about Psalm 27:3, "Though an army encamp against me, my heart does not fear;

Though war be waged against me, even then do I trust." Going into battle and not experiencing fear—could this love practice in our hearts be that powerful?

Ever since I was young, I've wanted to go parachuting. I literally have put it off for over forty years, due to the fear of death that I would imagine myself having when the plane door would open at seven thousand feet above the ground. So, I decided to test this synchronized breathing/heartbeat skill! I paid the fee with no fear. I went out to the tarmac and watched the previous group take off from the ground in the plane. The fear hit me, and I simply breathed it away in a minute or less. The fear came and was breathed away three times until my moment of truth. The plane door opened, only it was thirteen thousand feet above the ground, and I breathed the fear away from my heart in less than five seconds. I did this at age sixty-nine. I just breathed love to that drop and felt a spiritual release for the whole skydive. It was nothing short of wonderful.

If we are to love ourselves and to love others, then we need to approach life as a person with love emanating forth to God and to all creation. Otherwise, we limit our love experiences and capacities. We need to stay rooted and grounded in our origin: God, breathing life and love into the nostrils of our species; trusting us with this power of breathing. I believe that breathing coherently creates our natural God-given heartbeat. I believe this was the heartbeat of Adam and Eve in the Garden of Eden. It doesn't make sense that they would be in Paradise and have chaotic heartbeat patterns. Furthermore, when I'm in this natural, loving heartbeat—God created me to love; it's my nature—I find myself being more appreciative.

Now, what the Bible says is to bring peace and compassion to our hearts. I found that I am much more appreciative in my life of what's going on around me. Remember Colossians 3:12, "Put on then, as God's chosen ones, holy and beloved, heartfelt compassion, kindness, humility, gentleness, and patience." Elliott

(2006) states, "You can anticipate increased calm, comfort and sense of well-being." Breathing synchronously and coherently with the heart provides this ability to "put" these feelings "on" as the Bible states for us to do!

You know, a lot of us have been hurt by that word *love*. Maybe compassion, caring, and kindness can replace that hurt in such cases. It comes down to love. It wasn't love that hurt so many of us, even though the people who were doing the hurting might have been using that word. It wasn't love that created the psychological pain. Love feels kind and elicits strength within. It was the withdrawal of love that really hurt. Or perhaps it was the absence of love when it was dearly needed that hurt so much.

If we enter into this spirit of caring and kindness—imagine encountering a homeless beggar. If you're like me, I have thought, *He'll just use my donation to buy alcohol or drugs.* And sometimes I would think, *These guys are con artists, making big bucks begging.* Those thoughts come from my brain—when my heart feels frustrated, unhappy, or fearful. Notice how when the mind is in control, things seem chaotic, but when the heart directs our minds, the science has shown that the prefrontal cortex operates more efficiently. This is the part of the brain where we form judgments and make decisions. When I'm feeling compassion for that homeless beggar, then my heart directs my brain to think of what a pastor once said. "It's not about the drunk. It's about you," he said. "The issue is whether you are loving or indifferent."

Do I totally ignore the person? Or maybe I give him a gift card to a fast-food restaurant.

Mother Teresa endorsed thoughts like these with an engraving on the wall in her home in Calcutta, purportedly. I have a plaque with her advice that I once purchased. It says, "People are often unreasonable and self-centered. Forgive them anyway." In spite of what others do, we need to be kind. We need to strive for success, even when we're brought down. We need to be frank. We need to build things, even though they can be torn down. We can be happy when people don't want us to be happy. The good we do— people might forget it. The advice goes on and on with these kinds of ideas, but it ends this way: "For you see, in the end, it is between you and God. It never was between you and them anyway."

It's not just between me and that homeless beggar. It's between me and God! It's between me and love. He didn't say to feed the hungry unless they're addicted to drugs.

Another awkward moment—maybe you happen by and see a stranger crying. If you're like me, in the past I have stood there with a confused mind, wondering what to do. If I would just breathe compassion with my heart for the person crying, I just might go over there and place my hand upon his shoulder and let the subtle voice within my heart give power to my mind and express some kind words.

Some final biblical verses. Psalm 77:6 says, "At night I ponder in my heart; and as I meditate, my spirit probes."

Proverbs 2:2 says, "Turning your ear to wisdom, inclining your heart to understanding ..."

Proverbs 16:23 says, "The heart of the wise makes for eloquent speech, and increases the learning on their lips."

In the Catholic catechism it states in part IV, section 1, chapter 3, article 27:21 that in the Christian tradition there are three ways to pray. There is vocal prayer, meditation, and contemplative prayer. It's interesting to note that in all three forms of prayer the heart is mentioned. In terms of vocal prayer, article 27:22, "Vocal prayer, founded on the union of body and soul in human nature, associates the body with the interior prayer of the heart."

Meditation, in article 27:08, is described as necessary for the conversion of our hearts. And in contemplation, article 27:12, "But he knows that the love he is returning is poured out by the Spirit in his heart, for everything is grace from God."

The Spirit breathes. We breathe. God has a heart of love. We have a heart of love. And we have the abilities for our hearts to be loving and to emanate that love to God and to others.

A lot of people have hurts, psychological pains that will get in the way of practicing this. Many people don't have the discipline to just spend five minutes a day for three to four sessions, practicing this until it becomes a skill. If we do the technique regularly, however, we can use this technique to peel off layers of pain. We have layer, under layer, under layer of pain, just like the layers of an onion. These layers all make us cry like an onion makes us cry. And perhaps one of the biggest challenges in life is that we're probably the only species that knows that, inevitably, we are going to die.

So, if an animal is in a threatening situation, it fights it off—it's over; it's done with. He can go back to the homeostasis, synchronicity of the heart with nature. But a human being— we know that eventually, whatever that danger was, eventually, danger will overcome us. I wish we all had the answers to this core problem, but perhaps if we breathe love with our hearts, it will provide us with a path over a bridge back to Jesus, a path back to a loving heartbeat that perhaps Adam and Eve experienced.

Relaxed breathing with a focus upon the heart is a recurring theme for meditation. According to Michael Whelan, SM of the Aquinas Academy (2013), focusing upon the heart and upon breathing goes back to early Christianity. It was held in high regard by Thomas Merton, and is a primary focus of mysticism in the Greek tradition. St. Simeon (Day, 1954) is quoted as expressing:

> Sit down alone and in silence. Lower your head, shut your eyes, breathe out gently and imagine yourself looking into your own heart. As you breathe out, say "Lord Jesus Christ, have mercy on me." Say it moving your lips gently, or simply say it in your mind. Try to put all other thoughts aside. Be calm, be patient, and repeat the process very frequently.

Although these are instructions for the Jesus prayer, they describe putting oneself into a meditative state very well. Here, the use of the very similar technique that Elliott has found scientifically is meant for putting oneself into a state of love, peace, and compassion.

Bishop Fulton Sheen once said in one of his talks that love entails a surrendering, a surrendering of ourselves. Jesus gave himself totally to us. He trusted us so much. He trusted us even to his death. "Go ahead and kill me," is, in essence, what He seemed to say. "I will trust you, even that far." Can we love him back, no matter what? Perhaps, if the human race could do that as a whole, the end goal would bring us back to a Paradise where the lamb can lie down with the lion.

I want to quote the movie *The Pirates of the Caribbean III* here. Jack Sparrow, the captain of the ship, after all of his crazy meanderings, is told, "It's not about living forever, Jack. It's about living with yourself forever."

It's so simple. We just need to focus on synchronized breathing of five to six seconds in and five to six seconds out. We then focus on the inspirations God has given us to reinforce that pattern of breathing. Then, if we practice this for a short time, the brain and the body make the peace of God's Love automatic in our hearts. We can neutralize the stressors coming at us in society. It makes it so much easier to live with ourselves forever.

After death comes living forever. I want that living forever to be love for all humankind. My final quote is about heaven from Revelation 21:23–25: "The city had no need of sun or moon to shine on it, for the glory of God gave it light, and its lamp was the Lamb. The nations will walk by its light[s] and to it the kings of the earth will bring their treasure. During the day its gates will never be shut, and there will be no night there." Think of it! No more night. No more darkness. No more abyss. No more indifference to our needs for love. There will just be the radiant brilliance of the Light of the World, Love Himself, Jesus Christ! And we can enter into that light now through our hearts by breathing only love the way that He taught us!

REFERENCES

American Institute of Stress. Retrieved from http://www.stress.
org/ais-certified-organization-hm-library/ and http://
www.stress.org/certified-product-stress-eraser/

Apuleius (second century AD). *Metamorpheses*: Books IV-VI. In
The Encyclopaedia Britannica; Retrieved from http://www.
britannica.com/topic/Psyche-classical-mythology

Armour, J. & Ardell, J. (1984). *Neurocardiology*. New York, NY:
Oxford University Press.

Barks, C. (2003). *Rumi: the book of love: Poems of ecstasy and
longing*. New York, NY: Harper Collins Publishing.

Barlow, A. (1981). Gestalt-Antecedent Influence or Historical
Accident. *The Gestalt Journal, vol. IV Number 2.*

Battsek, John (Producer), & Bar-Lev, A. (Director). (2010). *The
Tillman Story* [motion picture]. United States: A&E Films.

Blakesee, S. (2006, January 10). Cells that read minds.
New York Times. Retrieved from: http://www.
nytimes.com/2006/01/10/science/10mirr.
html?pagewanted=all&_r=0

Brown, B. (2013) *The power of vulnerability: Teachings on authenticity, connection and courage.* Audible Audio Edition. Louisville, CO: Sounds True.

Brown, L., Acevedo, B., & Fisher, H. Neural Correlates of Four Broad Temperament Dimensions: Testing Predictions for a Novel Construct of Personality. *PLoS One, 8(11),* 1-8.

Bower, S.A. & Bower, G.H. (1991) *Asserting yourself: A practical guide for positive change.* Cambridge, MA: DeCapo Press.

Buscaglia, L. (1972). *Love.* New York, NY: Fawcett Crest.

Byrne, R. (2006). *The Secret.* New York, NY: Atria Books.

Calvo, R. (2014, December-2015, January). Teach. *High Desert Catholic* (Reno, NV).

Cannon, W. (1963). *Bodily changes in pain, hunger, fear and rage.* New York, NY: Branford, pp. 357 & 392.

Carel, H. (2015). *Born to be bad: Is Freud's death drive the source of human evilness?* Paper presented at UCLA. http://verakl.bol.ucla.edu/FR170X/Freud-death-drive.pdf

Carson, R. (1998). *The edge of the sea.* Wilmington, MA: Mariner Books—Houghton Mifflin Harcourt.

Childre, D. & Martin, H. (1999). *The Heartmath solution.* New York, NY: Harper Collins. p. 37.

Childre, D. & Rozman, (2005). *Transforming Stress: The heartmath solution for relieving worry, fatigue and tension.* Oakland, CA: New Harbinger Publications.

Christian Reference Bible Site, retrieved from http://www.
christianbiblereference.org/ faq_WordCount.htm

Cohen, R. (2013, April 30) Google glass: The next step in
computer evolution AND maybe even human evolution?
Forbes.

Crowd urges suicide leap by woman. (1973, September). *The
Phoenix Gazette.*

Danner, D., Snowden, D., & Frissen, W. (2001, May). Positive
emotions in early life and longevity: finding from the nun
study. *Journal of Personality and Social Psychology, 80(5),*
804-813.

Day, D. (1954) The Prayer of Jesus. *The Catholic Worker, Third
Hour #6.* Retrieved from: http://www.catholicworker.org/
dorothyday/ articles/883.html

De La Rochefoucauld, F. & Tancock, L. (1959). *Maxims.* New
York, NY: Penguin Group.

Elliott, S. & Edmonson, D. (2006). *The New Science of Breath.*
Allen, TX: Coherence Press.

Ellis, A. (1975). *A new guide to rational living.* Englewood Cliffs,
NJ: Prentice-Hall.

Einstein, A. Retrieved from http://www.goodreads.com/quotes/
search?utf8=%E2%9C%93&q= Einstein+life+miracle&
commit=Search

Erikson, E. *Childhood and society.* New York, NY: Norton, 1963,
p. 143.

Feeney, J., & Noller, P. (1990). Attachment style as a predictor of adult romantic relationships. *Journal of Personality and Social Psychology, 58,* 281-291.

Ferrer, E., Helm, J. L. (2012). Dynamical systems modeling of physiological coregulation in dyadic interactions. *International Journal of Psychophysiology.* DOI: 10.1016/j.ijpsycho.2012.10.013

Field, T., Hernandez-Reif, M., & Freedman, J. (2006). Prenatal, perinatal, and neonatal nurseries. *Infant Behavior and Development, 29,* 24-31.

Frankl, V.E. (1969). *The Will to Meaning.* New York, NY: Penguin Books, p. 23.

Frankl, V.E. (1965). *The Doctor and the soul: from psychotherapy to logotherapy.* (2nd ed.). (R. Winston & C. Winston, Trans.). New York, NY: Bantam Book. (Original work published 1946), 107-110.

Frankl, V. E. (1959). *Man's Search for Meaning: an introduction to logotherapy.* (I. Lasch, Trans.). New York, NY: Simon & Schuster Publishing. (Original work published 1959), 37.

Fredrickson, B. (1998, September). What good are positive emotions? *Review of General Psychology, 2*(3), 300–319.

Fromm, E. (1994). *Escape from freedom.* New York, NY: Holt Publishers.

Fromm, E. (1981). *Sane society.* New York, NY: Fawcett Publishing.

Fromm, E. (1956). *The Art of loving*. New York, NY: Harper & Row, p. 108.

Gelatt, H.B. & Gelatt, C. (2004). *Creative decision making using positive uncertainty*. Atascadero, CA: Impact Publishers.

Ghandi, M. Retrieved from http://www.goodreads.com/ quotes/22155-i-like-your-christ-i-do-not-like-your-christians

Gimpl G and Fahrenholz F. (2001) The oxytocin receptor system: structure, function, and regulation. Physiol Rev. Apr;81(2), 629-83. Retrieved from http://www.ncbi.nlm. nih.gov/ pubmed/11274341

Gregory, A., Cornell, D., Fan, X., Sheras, P., Shih, T., & Huang, F. (2010). Authoritative school discipline: High school practices associated with lower bullying and victimization. *Journal of Educational Psychology, 102*(2), 483.

Hadden, B. W., Smith, C.V., & Webster, G. D. (2014). Relationship duration moderates associations between attachments and relationship quality: Meta-analytic support for the temporal adult romantic attachment model. *Personality and Social Psychology Review, 18,* 42-58. (p.142)

Haidt, J. (2000) The positive emotion of elevation. *Prevention and treatment, 3*, article 3.

Harbaugh, W., Mayr, U., & Burghart, D. (2007) Neural responses to taxation and voluntary giving reveal motives for charitable donations. *Science, 316,* 1622-1625.

Harlow, H., Harlow, M., & Suomi, S. (1971). From thought to therapy: Lessons from a primate laboratory. *American Scientist, 59,* 538-549.

Harmon-Jones, E., Abramson, L., Sigelman, J., Bohlig, A., Hogan, M., & Harmon-Jones, C. (2002) Proneness to hypomania/mania symptoms or depression symptoms and asymmetrical frontal cortical responses to an anger-evoking event. *Journal of Personality and Social Psychology, 82*(4), 610-618.

James, W. (1890). *The principles of psychology* (Vol. 2). New York, NY, Holt.

Jung, C. G. (1962). *Symbols of Transformation: An Analysis of the Prelude to a Case of Schizophrenia* (Vol. 2, R. F. C. Hull, Trans.). New York: Harper & Brothers.

King, M.L. & Washington, J.M. (1991) *A Testament of Hope: The Essential Writings and Speeches of Martin Luther King, Jr.* New York: Harper Collins Publishers.

Krumboltz, J. & Levin, A.S. (2004). *Luck is no accident: Making the most of happenstance in your life and career.* Atascadero, CA: Impact Publishers.

LeDoux, J. (2002). *The Synaptic self.* London: Macmillan.

Lincoln, A. Retrieved from http://www. goodreads.com/quotes/ search?utf8 =%E2%9C%93&q=Lincoln+happy&commit=Search

Maslow, A. H. (1968). *Toward a psychology of being.* (2nd ed.). Princeton, NJ: D. Van Nostrand Co.

McWhirter, B. (1990). Loneliness: a review of current literature, with implications for counseling and research. *Journal of Counseling and Development, 68,* 417-422.

Mischel, W. & Ebbessen, E.B. (1970). Attention in delay of gratification. *Journal of Personality and Social Psychology, 16(2),* 339-337.

Miyamoto, Y. & Kitayama, S. (2002). Cultural variation in correspondence bias: the critical role of attitude diagnosticity of socially constrained behavior. *Journal of Personality & Social Psychology, 83(5),* 1239-1248.

Mob pelts cops halting suicide (1973, September). *Chicago Tribune,* Sec. 1—pp. 5

Morris, D. (1967). *The Naked ape: A zoologist's study of the human animal.* New York, NY: McGraw-Hill Publishing.

Mukaddam-Daher, S., Yin, Y., Roy, J., Gutkowska, J. & Cardinal, R. (2001, January). Negative inotropic and chronotropic effects of oxytocin. *American Heart Association Journals.* http://hyper.ahajournals.org/content/38/2/292.full.

Myers, D. (2014). *Exploring Psychology.* (9th ed.). New York, NY: Worth Publishers, p. 416.

Pascal, B. *Pascal's Pensee's.* http://oregonstate.edu/instruct/phl302/texts/pascal/pensees-contents.html 1670.

Pavlov, I. P. (1927). *Conditioned Reflexes: An Investigation of the Physiological Activity of the Cerebral Cortex. Translated and Edited by G. V. Anrep. London: Oxford University Press.*

Poe, E.A. (1849). *A Dream within a Dream*. http://www. poetryfoundation.org/poems-and-poets/poems/detail/52829

Powell, John. (1969). *Why am I afraid to tell you who I am?* Chicago, IL: Argus Communications Co., 49.

Rodin, J. (1996) Aging and health: Effects of the sense of control. *Science*, 233. Pgs. 1271-1276.

Rubin, E (1921) *Visnell Wahngenommene Figuren: Studien in psychologischer analyse.* Kobenhavn: Gyldendalske Boghandel.

Salovey, P. (1990). Interview. *American Scientist.* Jan./Feb., 25-29.

Seiden, L. S. (2013, February 26). Buckminster Fuller: a verb who supported all life on spaceship earth. *The Huffington Post.*

Seligman, M. (1975). *Helplessness: On depression, development and death.* San Francisco: Freeman.

Seligman, M., Steen, T., Park, N., & Peterson, C. (2005) Positive psychology progress: empirical validation of interventions. *American Psychologist, 60,* 410-421.

Sharkin, B. S. (2004). Road Rage: Risk factors, assessment, and intervention strategies. *Journal of Counseling & Development, 82(2),* 191.

Shoda, Y., Mischel, W., & Peake, P.K. (1990). Predicting adolescent cognitive and self-regulating competencies from preschool delay of gratification: Identifying diagnostic conditions. *Developmental Psychology, 26(6):* 978-986.

Sills, J. (2007). Love at work. *Psychology Today, 40(2),* 64-65.

Sternberg, R. (1986). A triangular theory of love. *Psychological Review, 93,* 119-135.

Titchener, E.B. (1910). *Textbook of psychology.* New York: Macmillan.

Tremmel, P. (Oct. 27, 2009) Culture of We Buffers Genetic Tendency to Depression. University of Northwestern News. Retrieved from http://www.northwestern.edu/ newscenter/stories /2009/ 10/chiao.html#sthash.zlwrJfdC. dpuf

United Press International. (1967, October 15). Shunned Negro hero would trade publicity for "five good friends." *The Modesto Bee,* p. 4.

Van der Kolk, B. (2013). *Treatment of individual with PTSD and comorbid psychiatric: A constructive narrative.* Paper presented at the 2013 Evolution of Psychotherapy Conference.

Van der Kolk, B. and Saporta, J. (1991) The Biological Response to Psychic Trauma: Mechanisms and Treatment of Intrusion and Numbing. *Anxiety Research,* vol. 4, 199-212.

Wagoner, David. An old Native American elder story rendered into modern English by David Wagoner, in *The Heart Aroused—Poetry and the Preservation of the Soul in Corporate America* by David Whyte, Currency Doubleday, New York, 1996.

Wall, Chuck. (July, 2016). The KINDNESS Keynote
    Presentation. Retrieved from http://www.chuckwall.net/
    topics.htm

Whelan, Michael. (2013) *An Introduction to the Jesus Prayer.*
    Retrieved from http://www. aquinas-academy.com/2014-
    01-15-23-49-43/essays/michael-whelan-sm/122-an-
    introduction-to-the-jesus-prayer

Younger, J., Aron, A., Parke, S., Chatterjee, N., & Mackey, S.
    (2010). Viewing pictures of a romantic partner reduces
    experimental pain: involvement of neural reward
    systems. PL$_o$S ONE 5(10): e13309. Doi:101371/journal.
    pone.0013309. Pg. 365.

Printed in the United States
By Bookmasters